PRAISE FOR *STAND OUT AS A THOUGHT LEADER*

// Understand. Do the work. Stand out with purpose.
Combining sense and sensibility, *Stand Out as a Thought Leader* pushes the envelope to capture a wider audience for thought leaders. It provides innovative ways to inspire others to promote cooperation and growth. How they distill down the eight fundamentals is brilliant and incredibly relevant for those looking to stand out. If you are a business leader, what are you waiting for? Get this book, learn how to lead with purpose, and make a positive impact in your world.
—**SCOTT C. MALONEY** – President, K2M Design, Inc., K2MDesign.com

// *Stand Out as a Thought Leader* is an operational and pragmatic approach to evolving as a thought leader. The assessments, lists, and tools are easily applied and utilized and are highly relevant to modern leadership development. This book is not just frameworks or suggestions, but instead contains real, action-oriented systems that are ideal for entrepreneurs and others looking to make an impact.
—**MARC O. STOCKLI** – Partner, MOS Advisory Services & Global Chair, Board of Directors, Entrepreneurs' Organization

// Leadership has never been more important than it is today. Business leaders are expected to promote positive change and we need a book that captures the true driver of such changes—purpose! With an authenticity-centered leadership style, you'll be able make your mark on this world by focusing less about making profits at any cost but rather using them as fertilizer for growth in ways which will create long-term impactful benefits beyond maximizing returns alone.
—**KATE HANCOCK** – Founder, Metaverse XYZ, Metaverse-XYZ.com

// Whether you like it or not, like death and taxes, everyone now has a personal brand. The question is, what are you going to do with it? Are you going to let the outside world "brand" you or are you going to stand out and brand yourself? *Stand Out as a Thought Leader* is an authentic and relevant message designed to help you stand out from the crowd and brand yourself so you can make the biggest impact possible.
—**MARC GUTMAN** – Brand Strategist, Wildstory, Wildstory.com

// As a busy entrepreneur or business executive it can feel overwhelming and hard to start the journey to authentic thought leadership. This book is a true North Star for any leader wanting to stand out, launch and stay on course on their personal branding journey.
—**KIM WHITAKER** – Entrepreneur

// In this crowed over-communicated world we live in, standing out from the crowd can be difficult. *Stand Out as a Thought Leader* provides a guide on how to achieve it. It is written by proven communication experts who have used this process repeatedly. If you are serious about making a difference and standing out, this is your bible.
—**DAVID ANDERSON** – Founder & CEO Off Madison Ave & LighthousePE. Immediate Past Chair, Entrepreneurs' Organization, OffMadisonAve.com, LighthousePE.ai

// The main paradigm change in today's leadership mindset is serving instead of guiding others. This shift is about devotion to people and causes, beyond oneself. This book will provide you the tools for a mindset change for leaders like you, devoted to working and living their purpose.
—**DR. ENRIQUE PRESBURGER** – CEO, Factor Exprés, Financial Institution, Enrique-Presburger.com

// The ability to understand and define your own purpose as a leader is only the first step in standing out amongst all the voices of leaders that we hear every day. *Stand Out as a Thought Leader* pushes you, an aspiring thought leader, to answer the question, "What is your purpose?", and then supplies you with the tools you need to build upon that answer. This guide is a lifeline for the modern thought leader.
—**DANIELLA MENACHEMSON** – President, StyleNations, StyleNations.com

// This is the most accessible and compressed work on how you can stand out as a thought leader. When you want your message, that lives inside you, to be heard by the right audience, read this book.
—**WENDY VAN IERSCHOT** – CEO, VIE People, WendyVanIerschot.com

// I believe that entrepreneurs are the driving force of change and innovation and our world today. They provide jobs, economic growth, products and services that change peoples' lives everyday. *Stand Out as a Thought Leader* helps entrepreneurs find their voice so they can reach more people and do more good, while becoming the leader they were meant to be.
—**JESSICA FIALKOVICH** – President, Exit Factor, ExitFactor.com

// *Stand Out as a Thought Leader* brings to mind a poem from Marianne Williamson. In that poem, Williamson inspires us to shine, to be liberated, not holding back. By shining, we inspire people around us to do the same, creating a ripple effect of positive authentic impact in the world. Using this book as a guide, one will shine and unleash their purpose, creating a ripple effect of positive impact in the world.
—**CHANG NG** – Founder and Chairman, Constrive Group, Constrive.com

// As an entrepreneur, *Stand Out as a Thought Leader* is an essential piece in my library. The practical tools and carefully detailed steps combine to create the perfect handbook, helping business leaders define their authentic purpose. With this blueprint in hand, anyone ready to put the time, effort, and passion into developing as a thought leader, will be able to do it.
—**ANDREA HERRERA** – President/Founder, Amazing Edibles Catering/Boxperience, CaterAmazing.com

// *Stand Out as a Thought Leader* is a simple, easy-to-understand, authentic guide to a leader's journey of discovering purpose, using your internal navigation system and taking decisive action steps to put forth a strong brand. It provides a clear path, shining a light on each of the 8 fundamentals with specific considerations, making the reader reflect on where they are at, where they need to be, and how to get there whilst still being true to their purpose. The reader is left excited about chartering a new course with a clear map. Every leader and entrepreneur should have this map to start their journey or as a check point along the way.
—**SASKIA H. HILL** – CEO and Founder, Connect BPS, ConnectBPS.com

// Self-awareness and consistency are two of the most important things you could have as a brand. And your brand, well that's the most important thing you can have. Having a guidebook like *Stand Out as a Thought Leader* is crucial as I believe everyone should build the foundations of who they are and what they represent. It will also make the good ones become the best.
—**NIR ZAVARO** – Chief of Happiness, Streetwise, NirZavaro.com

// *Stand Out as a Thought Leader.* This book gives you all the tools you need to be a thought leader. It is so important for women to stand up and walk into your power as a thought leader. This book will help you find the tools to identify, nurture and share that power. Enjoy this book and claim your power as a thought leader.
—**DR. KRISTIN L KAHLE** – Founder, NavigateHCR, DrKristinKahle.com

// Now, more than ever, the world needs authentic leaders who know their purpose, speak their truth, and have the courage to lead. If that's you—if you're looking to find your voice, *Stand Out as a Thought Leader* is the road map that can help you get there.
—**STEVE SATTERWHITE** – CEO, Entelligence, Entelligence.com

// With all the pressure on leaders caused by the current state of affairs in the world, it is easy to get distracted from the idea that you need to spread leadership ideas amongst your team, peers and community. Part of leadership is willingly sharing what you know in order to help the next generation of leaders. Having a step-by-step guide like *Stand Out as a Thought Leader* offers a framework to support leaders in achieving their potential.
—**JOE GALATAS** – President, McDonough Elevator Sales & Rentals, ONEMcDonough.com

// The writers have captured the true essence of positioning your personal brand as a leader. Reputation, authenticity & the color you choose as a leader is how you shape your own brand personality. The choices you consciously make determine who you stand for as a leader. This will ultimately narrate your story differently.
—**SHARAN J. VALIRAM** – Executive Director, Valiram, Valiram.com

// Although we've been in business for over 10 years I had never taken the necessary step to understand our true authenticity. Reading *Stand Out as a Thought Leader* really changed my mindset, helping me understand that we need to stand for more than just the business we are in and the services we deliver. *Stand Out as a Thought Leader* provides that thought-provoking road map to determining your distinct advantage and becoming a true thought leader. It's an eye-opening journey for both you personally and your organization.
—**DARYL EIFLER** – Founder/CEO, i4COLOR, i4COLORinc.com

// This book is a wonderful guide for people to follow and amplify your current leadership and brand. Written by true thought leaders who walk their talk. A must read if you're ready to take immediate action.
—**LISA ANDREWS** – CEO, WAVIA, Wavia.global

// *Stand Out as a Thought Leader* is the essence of finding who you are, what you do, and most importantly why you do it. Almost going through bankruptcy of my first business in my early 40s, I realized that it is so important to align your soul, mind, and actions. I needed this book 5 years ago so I could have saved my time. This is not the book to keep on the shelf, but to keep it as a bible daily, weekly, and annually.
—**NOBI FUJITA** – President, Seibu Shoko Co., Ltd, SeibuShoko.com

STAND OUT
AS A
THOUGHT
LEADER

Published by:

// TwinEngine™

© 2022 Winnie Hart

Book design: Winnie Hart and Moe Lee
Book editor: William Guion

Imprint of TwinEngine
TwinEngine.com

ISBN: 978-0-9968389-1-7 (HC)
ISBN: 978-0-9968389-3-1 (SC)
ISBN: 978-0-9968389-2-4 (eBook)
Printed in the United States of America
First Edition

TO ALL OF THE
THOUGHT LEADERS
OUT THERE WHO
HAVE A MESSAGE
WE NEED TO HEAR

THIS BOOK IS **DIVIDED BY THE 8 FUNDAMENTALS OF STANDING OUT AS A THOUGHT LEADER.** YOU CAN READ FROM START TO FINISH OR **JUMP TO THE FUNDAMENTAL** YOU NEED TO STRENGTHEN.

STAND OUT

THE 8 FUNDAMENTALS

TAKE OFF

STAY ON COURSE

GET STARTED TODAY

RESOURCES

STRATEGY

REPU**T**ATION

AUDIENCE

AUTHE**N**TICITY

I**D**ENTITY

TOOLS TO MASTER THE 8 FUNDAMENTALS OF
STANDING OUT AS A THOUGHT LEADER

DISTINCTI**O**N

P**U**RPOSE

MINDSE**T**

DEAR LEADER,

More than ever, the world needs you to **STAND OUT AS A THOUGHT LEADER** and live your purpose. People, like you, with innovative ideas can help meet the challenges and problems facing society and business today. We need your imaginative thinking and more effective solutions to inspire others, promote cooperation and growth, and infuse new energy into outdated systems and processes. **THE WORLD NEEDS THOUGHT LEADERS WHO CAN LEAD FROM THE HEART AS WELL AS THE HEAD,** leaders who are human, empathetic, yet unafraid of being who they are and speaking the truth of what they know—**LEADERS**

WHO ARE DEVOTED TO WORKING AND LIVING THEIR PURPOSE, focused on tackling the big issues of our time, and willing to share their talents and expertise to create a better world. **WHERE WILL THOSE LEADERS COME FROM?** We believe you are already out there. Your voices and ideas are simply not being heard by a wide audience—**YET.** In small entrepreneurial businesses and large corporations, these new thought leaders are sharing their ideas, products or services, and striving to reach a larger audience. Are you willing to take a stand and stand out? **THE WORLD NEEDS YOU.**

IF YOU ANSWER **"YES"** TO ANY OF THESE QUESTIONS **THIS BOOK IS FOR YOU.**

DO YOU KNOW WHAT QUALITIES MAKE YOU TRULY DISTINCT? Do you want to make a real difference in the world? **DO YOU KNOW YOUR PURPOSE AND THE IMPACT YOU MAKE?** Are you willing to take a stand and stand out? **DO YOU HAVE A STORY TO SHARE BUT DON'T KNOW EXACTLY HOW?**

THIS IS AN INVITATION
TO DISCOVER THE
THOUGHT LEADER
YOU ARE MEANT TO BE.

THE IMPORTANCE OF STANDING OUT AS A THOUGHT LEADER

Who is a thought leader? Quite simply a thought leader could be anyone with the passion, dedication and perseverance to follow an idea that captures their imagination and the desire to share that idea with others.

You can find potential thought leaders almost everywhere—in your family, your circle of friends, at work and at play. They may have an original viewpoint on a subject or concern that captures their interest and fuels their passion. So, they pursue that subject because they feel it's important and necessary. Sometimes, their ideas start movements or businesses. Sometimes, their ideas lead to solutions and answers to the big questions and challenges of our time.

These potential thought leaders explore and pursue their area of interest until eventually other people begin to recognize that their message has value. They may be considered experts or authorities in their field. They're often not satisfied with just discussing their ideas; they want to influence others, not just in their field, but for society and even the world.

Today, we need these thought leaders to expand their potential and expose their ideas and solutions to a wider audience. The need has never been more critical for the future of society, cultures, the economy, and the world.

Today, simply standing for something is not the only thing that matters, it's about making an impact, as well as stepping up and encouraging others to make a difference too. Because as we see it, the future is about growing communities. Look around and you can see it happening already. People with similar interests and goals are gathering and working together to promote innovative solutions for the challenges facing us. And at the heart of these communities are potential thought leaders, inspiring individuals who are focused on positive change.

We know this is true because we speak with emerging leaders and consult with them every day in our business. We believe that when you know what you stand for and what makes you unique—as a person, as a leader, as an entrepreneur, as a speaker, and as a thought leader, you will create the alignment and the momentum to achieve anything. You are unstoppable.

This book offers a new perspective and a clear and structured approach to mastering the ability to **STAND OUT** as a leader in your field, to be remembered, and become a trusted thought leader, with answers to today's tough questions. It contains directions to help leaders (like you) identify what you stand for, what qualities make you truly unique, and to discover what inspires you and how you can inspire others. You'll learn how to grow an audience, influence trends, and encourage innovation and growth.

Within these pages you will learn about the 8 fundamental areas that can help you identify your distinct advantage and create a strategy to communicate "What You Stand For" so you can **STAND OUT** from the crowd.

You'll explore the importance of **Purpose, Reputation, Identity, Authenticity, Audience, Distinction, Strategy and Mindset**—8 fundamentals of standing out paired with diagnostic assessments and exercises that will help you identify your Distinct Advantage—the talents, qualities and values that define who you are as an individual—and show you how to leverage that advantage to **STAND OUT** as the thought leader you are meant to be.

BE WHO YOU ARE, ONLY MORE SO.

At TwinEngine we've seen people and brands for more than three decades who believed the misguided idea that the next flashy advertising campaign would propel them to a higher level of recognition and profit.

But the simple (and unflashy) formula for shaping a brand that stands out is this: to be more of who and what you already are. Then, learn to communicate that truthfully and authentically to your audience. Why? Because authenticity is sustainable. It builds trust and attracts followers. Authenticity is the way of the future.

You stand out when you **KNOW WHAT YOU STAND FOR** and live your distinct advantage.

People recognize and value honesty, simplicity and integrity. They are attracted to it and reward it with their loyalty. When you're not authentic, an audience can tell. And in today's online, real-time environment, if you don't tell the truth, someone else surely will. People also value clarity. They want to know what it is about you, your experience and your expertise that is of value to them and their lives.

My sister, Lorrie, and I are identical twins. We are the twins at TwinEngine. Being identical twins, we know a lot about the confusion and frustration that comes from a lack of clarity when things look the same. Until our late teens, we were known as one person "Winnie-Lorrie" (that's one word) or "The Little Twins." It has taught us a simple truth about differences. When you look at identical twins, what do you think?

How are they different?

What makes each of them unique?

Identical twins are intriguing—because people usually can't tell them apart.

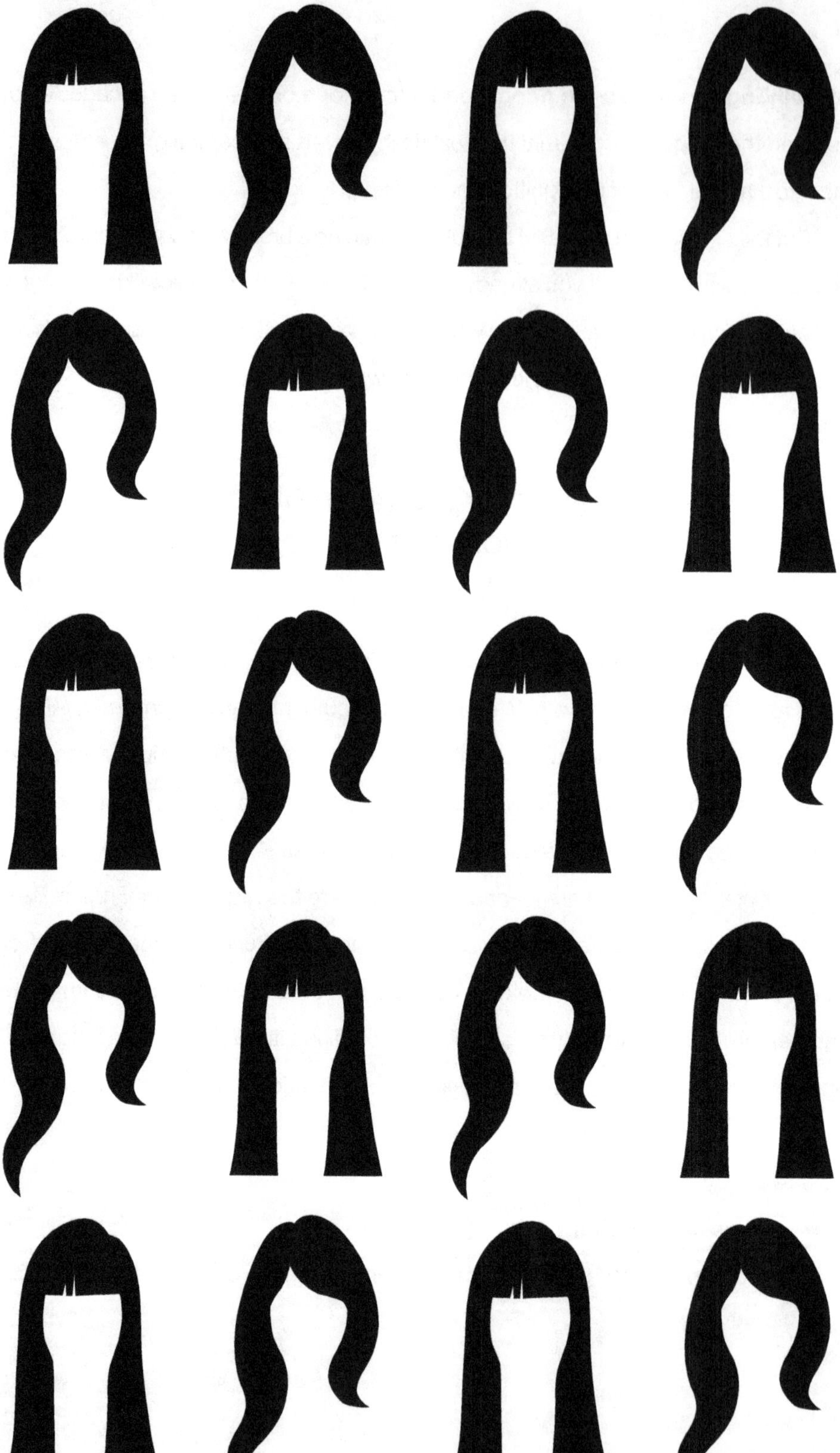

We live in a world that appreciates and expects individual differences in appearance and behavior. So, when we encounter two identical individuals (like Lorrie and me), this experience challenges our beliefs about the way that the world works.

Of course, identical twins are never exactly alike, and some differ in profound ways. Yet we can't stop ourselves from comparing them and trying to find the differences that help us to tell them apart. **By taking a closer look at twins, we can learn a great deal about the concept of differentiation.** By looking past what's just intriguing, we can learn about how we perceive differences in anyone or anything.

When I look at my twin, I can experience how others view me—and actually see me from outside of myself.

DISCOVERING EXACTLY HOW YOU ARE DIFFERENT IS YOUR CHALLENGE.

I've learned firsthand to identify and appreciate what makes us different. There are physical differences and there are inner differences—one of us is a left-brain thinker and one is a right-brain thinker. One is creative and expressive, the other is rational and linear. But it's the pairing and integration of these different qualities that makes our brand agency, TwinEngine, what it is. It's our distinct advantage: right brain, left brain, creative and analytic. And when the two work together as one, the whole is greater than the individual parts. From firsthand experience at refining our individuality throughout our lives, we've perfected the ability to perceive distinct differences in other people, other companies and other brands.

TO STAND OUT, YOU MUST
BE MORE OF WHAT MAKES
YOU WHO YOU ARE—
**THOSE INNER VALUES,
PASSIONS, TALENTS,
AND EXPERIENCES**—THE
POSITIVE QUALITIES THAT
PEOPLE ALREADY RECOGNIZE
AND APPRECIATE. **YOUR
CHALLENGE IS TO IDENTIFY
THOSE THINGS, NURTURE
THEM, SHARE THEM, AND
PROMOTE THEM**—THEY ARE
YOUR DISTINCT ADVANTAGE
AND THE SOURCE OF
YOUR SUCCESS.

HOW THIS BOOK WILL HELP YOU STAND OUT, TAKE OFF, AND STAY ON COURSE.

Being more of who and what you are may sound like a simple idea, but the process of applying this concept to become a thought leader is more complex. That's why we created this book. Here's a tip to get the most from what we've written.

We believe that each of us has a built-in navigation system—an accumulation of all that we've learned or know intuitively—that works like a compass to point us toward our truth (authenticity) and highest potential. Throughout this book we'll talk about the importance of leveraging our personal authenticity to know what's true for each of us.

Truth and authenticity, in the sense that we use those terms here, are largely personal matters. You know better than anyone what's true for you. You sense when you're on course and when you're off. So, as you go through the sections and exercises in how to *Stand Out As A Thought Leader*, read with your navigation system turned on and tuned in. That way you'll feel what's true and relevant for you and take away the parts that will best serve your growth.

// STAND OUT
Strengthen The 8 Fundamentals of standing out as a thought leader—purpose, reputation, identity, authenticity, audience, distinction, strategy and mindset—to attract a larger audience and increase followers.

// TAKE OFF
Build a strategy and plan of action to communicate what makes you unique that aligns with your goals. Define the most effective tools that will get you off the tarmac the fastest.

// STAY ON COURSE
Execute a system that keeps you moving in the right direction. Measure results and plan for more of what delivers the best results.

The sections of this book explore The 8 Fundamentals that we've determined are essential to clarifying your brand and developing your full potential. Though any individual can benefit from the information presented here, most of those with whom we work have already realized that something is missing or lacking in their efforts. They're working hard, but the gap between where they are and where they want to be isn't shrinking.

This book can help change that. The concepts and exercises contained in these pages are structured to uncover what is missing from your efforts. We have even seen this system provide just the inspiration and momentum an emerging leader needs to make a huge leap forward in performance and recognition.

SO, LET'S GET STARTED . . .

Before you can take steps to Stand Out, you need to identify where you are. Our Brand Traffic Control system is designed to do just that. Through a series of diagnostic questions, we'll pinpoint problem areas and uncover opportunities to help focus on what next steps are right for you—for where you are now and where you want to go.

IDENTIFY YOUR CHALLENGES

CHALLENGES EXERCISE: Utilize this checklist as an exercise to evaluate what areas need strengthening and to prioritize key initiatives.

// STAND OUT:

- ☐ I have a message but don't know how to share it
- ☐ I need to communicate my purpose clearly
- ☐ I don't know what makes me unique
- ☐ I need to build my personal brand
- ☐ I want to reach a bigger audience
- ☐ I need to position myself as a leader in my field
- ☐ I want to stand out in my field
- ☐ I want to make a bigger impact

// TAKE OFF:

- ☐ I need a next-level strategy to build my brand
- ☐ I need to focus my message to reach a broader audience
- ☐ I have stalled and need a plan to take off
- ☐ I need a consistent presence in my field
- ☐ I want to grow at a faster pace
- ☐ I need to align my goals and growth strategies

// STAY ON COURSE:

- ☐ I have drifted off course and need to realign
- ☐ I need a plan to measure what works and what doesn't
- ☐ I need to meet regularly to ensure that I am aligned
- ☐ I need a 12-month strategic plan
- ☐ I need a focused mindset

IDENTIFY YOUR CHALLENGES

CHALLENGES SUMMARY: Record your top 5 challenges and your number 1 challenge.

// NUMBER 1 CHALLENGE:

// TOP 5 CHALLENGES:

BY FOCUSING ON, PRACTICING AND MASTERING THESE FUNDAMENTALS YOU WILL **STAND OUT, TAKE OFF AND STAY ON COURSE.**

THE EIGHT

The order in which The 8 Fundamentals are presented in this book is not necessarily how you will or should use them in your personal development. Each leader has different strengths and needs and is at a different place. You should work with the fundamentals in the order that best serves your growth.

PURPOSE
REPUTATION
IDENTITY
AUTHENTICITY

AUDIENCE
DISTINCTION
STRATEGY
MINDSET

From our experience, we have determined eight primary areas that contribute to standing out as a thought leader. We've distilled what we've learned into The 8 Fundamentals defined below. Ideally, this information will help you to shine a light on shortcomings or challenges in your strategy and provide suggestions and solutions for you to Stand Out as a leader, Take Off in a direction that's true to who you are and where you want to be, and to Stay On Course to reach your goals.

PURPOSE You know and live your purpose;
you know what you stand for and are true to your core beliefs.

REPUTATION There is continuous and ongoing awareness
of your reputation and other trending ideas and topics.

IDENTITY The outward appearance of your brand truly reflects
who you are and the value you deliver.

AUTHENTICITY Your messaging is consistent, true,
genuine and communicates your key message.

AUDIENCE You have a consistent flow of new followers
who you can define, identify, nurture and manage.

DISTINCTION You stand out in the field of competing ideas,
influencers and other thought leaders.

STRATEGY A 12-month strategic plan is in force and
aligned with your goals.

MINDSET You are focused and committed to achieve desired results.

FROM OUR EXPERIENCE
WE HAVE FOUND THESE
8 FUNDAMENTALS
CONTRIBUTE MOST
TO **STANDING OUT**
AS A THOUGHT LEADER.

BRAND TRAFFIC CONTROL

It's a big sky out there—and emerging leaders can get overwhelmed trying to keep track of how and if their own message is heard and preferred by their audience. How can you know with any certainty if you are on course or lost among dozens of competing ideas or peers?

Leaders can't always direct the conversation about who they are or what they say in the way they could before online and social media conversations existed. Traditional market research must be combined with active listening and monitoring of what's being said or written about you. Today, a dialogue is the optimum solution.

Your brand (how you are perceived) is shaped by your audience—by the people commenting on or recommending you and the ideas or solutions you promote. People who like and endorse you on social media can be important brand ambassadors and make a significant impact on existing and potential followers. But do you have the tools to influence and direct the conversation?

When you strengthen The 8 Fundamentals, you will stand out, know where you are relative to other thought leaders, and know how to create consistent messaging to increase audience engagement. Your brand will be aligned with who you are, you'll be able to execute plans more effectively, you'll understand what makes your brand distinct, you'll have tools to measure what's working and what isn't, and you'll be able to positiion yourself to take off.

LOCATE YOUR CURRENT POSITION

To discover what you need to do to stand out using the Brand Traffic Control radar, you need to know where you currently rate on each of the fundamental brand attributes and how aligned you and your team are in the perception of where your organization stands on each.

BRAND TRAFFIC CONTROL RADAR

This Brand Traffic Control Radar assessment tool graphically plots the status of The 8 Fundamentals that are key to your success. Using definitions for each fundamental as outlined earlier in this section, consider your current position within each indicator. Scale: zero in the center (non-existing) to five on the outside ring (highest level). Go to StandOutasaThoughtLeader.com to download the tool.

If you don't **KNOW WHERE YOU ARE GOING,** you'll never get there.

WHAT'S ON YOUR RADAR?

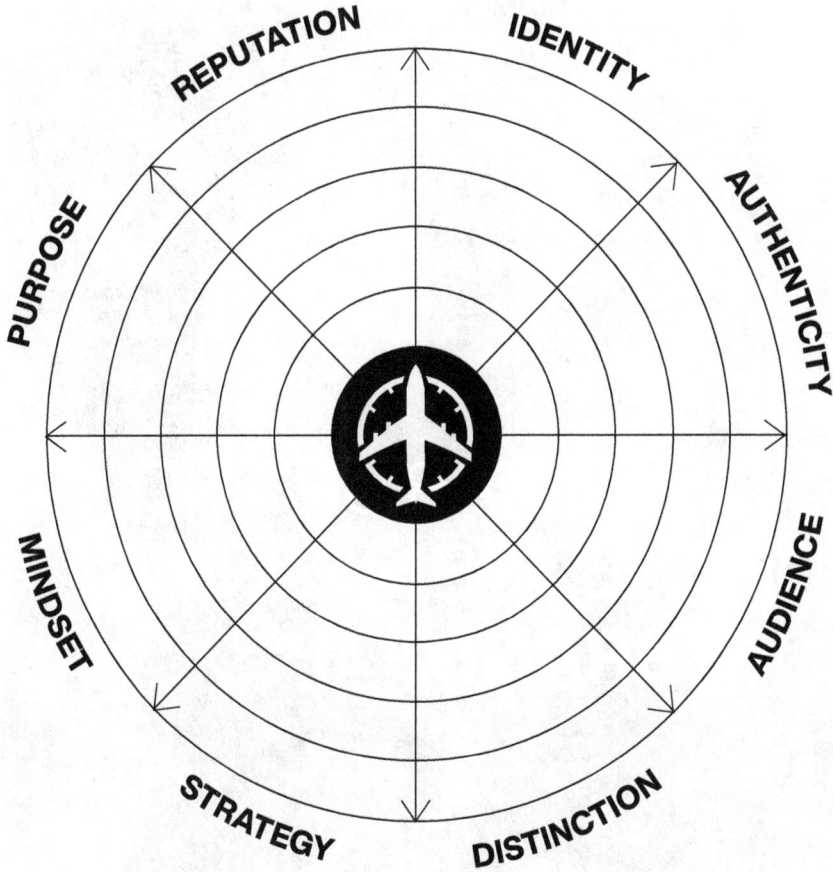

Brand Traffic Control (BTC) Radar Exercise:

Go to StandOutasaThoughtLeader.com to download the radar to plot your

opinion of your current position within each indicator on a scale of zero in the center

(non-existent) to five on the outside ring (highest level).

WHAT'S IN AND WHAT'S OUT

The field of branding is no stranger to disruption. As the world of communications change so will the opportunities for creating and growing brands.

WHAT'S IN	WHAT'S OUT
ONE-TO-ONE Targeted to the individual	**MASS MARKETING** Targeted to everyone
REAL Human to human	**ROBOTIC** Perfectly choreographed
MICRO FOCUS Real-time and where you are	**BROAD FOCUS** Marketing to the masses
DIALOGUE Two-way conversation	**MONOLOGUE** One-way marketing
BEHAVIORAL Understands your needs	**MECHANICAL** Unemotional
SOCIAL PLATFORMS Conversational	**STATIC WEBSITES** Informational

EIGHT ATTRIBUTES OF THE WORLD'S MOST MEMORABLE BRANDS

1. The brand is consistent.

A strong thought leader's brand maintains a successful balance between continuity and change. A strong brand is consistent with its message of benefits through promotional campaigns and to varying audiences. It avoids creating confusion or sending conflicting messages about who it is or what it does.

2. The brand reflects an individual's core values.

A thought leader should be an extension of what he or she stands for and believes in, those essential principles that guide their activities, operations, and relationships. Core values help followers understand a leader's personality and build trust in the brand and what it stands for.

3. The brand maintains its relevancy over time.

With strong brands, equity is a dynamic attribute. It's tied to the actual quality of a thought leader's work, the longevity of their message, as well as other intangible aspects that may change over time.

4. The brand uses a full range of marketing and communications activities to build brand equity.

A strong individual brand uses all the elements associated with a business or product brand—logos, symbols, slogans, books, products, offerings and signage to enhance and reinforce followers' awareness of the brand over time. They use these elements consistently across multiple media and online, in all communications and promotions, through sponsorships and through endorsements to spread recognition and build awareness of the individual's brand.

5. The brand does an excellent job of delivering the thought leader's message.

Why do individuals follow a thought leader? It's not just because of the appeal of his or her message, but also because of the brand image, reputation, trustworthiness, authenticity, and several other factors. This unified impression in the followers' minds is what influences loyalty and audience growth. A brand with a favorable impression becomes a trusted asset and an extension of their followers' lifestyle or personality.

6. The brand is properly positioned against its peers.

When a brand is well positioned, it fills a particular niche in its followers' minds. That's because the brand has worked hard over time to build and maintain its niche in the public's awareness by emphasizing its distinct differentiators.

7. The thought leader monitors various media sources to manage their brand equity.

Strong brands conduct regular checkups and brand-tracking studies to determine the health of the brand's identity. This may consist of a detailed review of how the elements of the brand have been used in all marketing and communications during the recent past. It may also be done externally through consumer focus groups, online data and surveys.

8. The brand is given adequate resource support and that support is sustained over the long run.

Brand equity is built carefully and intentionally over time by sustained brand awareness.

(This information was adapted from: The Brand Report Card by Kevin Lane Keller published in Harvard Business Review)

WHAT DOES THAT MEAN TO YOU?

How do these attributes of strong brands help you? As stated at the beginning of this book, a familiar recognizable brand can get noticed and remembered. When your brand as a thought leader is strong and aligned, it pays you in dividends—greater audience numbers, higher audience awareness, and more loyal followers. When your brand is weak and out of alignment, it's like driving a car when the wheels are out of alignment. It might get you where you want to go, and then again it might not.

How much of your resources are dedicated to building your personal brand? Your brand is like an investment. It needs to have a strategy, goals, regular check-ups and a maintenance program to stay strong and growing.

Think of your brand as a primary asset.

When you look at your daily calendar, how much time do you invest in building your brand? Each month? Or even each week?

- ☐ 5 hours
- ☐ Weekly
- ☐ Monthly

- ☐ 10 hours
- ☐ Weekly
- ☐ Monthly

- ☐ 20 hours
- ☐ Weekly
- ☐ Monthly

- ☐ 30 hours
- ☐ Weekly
- ☐ Monthly

YOUR AUDIENCE IS INTERESTED IN "WHY YOU DO WHAT YOU DO" AS MUCH AS "WHAT YOU DO AND SAY." WHO YOU ARE AND WHAT YOU STAND FOR WILL NEED TO BE CLEARLY DEFINED. SUCCESSFUL BRANDS FOCUS ON LIVING THE BRAND. **YOU MUST BE ABLE TO COMMUNICATE YOUR MESSAGE AND MISSION.**

INVESTING IN BRAND EQUITY

Though a brand is an intangible "thing," marketing researchers believe that it is one of the most important things you own. The image, personality, name recognition, identity, reputation and positive attitudes associated with you and the relevancy and usefulness of your ideas or solutions are referred to as your brand equity. It is the extra value that influences an individual's decision to become a follower.

And regardless of the methods used to measure brand equity, all researchers agree that strong, well-leveraged brands and brand awareness have the potential to positively impact a leader's perceived value and growth potential.

Throughout this book, we feature thought leaders that stand out.
Look for the stars for inspiration.

// BRENÉ BROWN
Brené Brown stands out as a thought leader because she debunks many of the ideas that others hold about fear and risk. She deals directly and openly with emotional vulnerability and believes that vulnerability is the origin of love, belonging, joy, courage, empathy and creativity. It is the door to all of the emotions and experiences we crave.

Brené Brown's Stand Out Statement:

Vulnerability is the core, the heart, the center of meaningful human experience.

STAND FOR SOMETHING AND YOU'LL STAND OUT.

In today's environment, standing out and being noticed and remembered by your audiences and followers is not only crucial, it's a matter of success or failure.

After years of working with various leaders and brands, we learned that the most effective strategy in standing out is to first identify who you are (your authentic self) and why you do what you do (your purpose) and then integrate these into every part of your public persona (your brand).

If you were asked the question, "Why do you do what you do?" your first thought may be, "To share what I know with others, of course." All thought leaders need to grow their audiences, to be heard and recognized. But in today's over-congested mediascape, offering a new idea or solution isn't enough to stand out. You need a laser focus on your message and your personal brand to rise above the crowd.

WHY DO INDIVIDUALS FOLLOW A THOUGHT LEADER?

It's not just because of the appeal of his or her message, but also because of the brand image, reputation, trustworthiness, authenticity, and several other factors.

WHERE DOES YOUR BRAND STAND NOW?

One of the steps in standing out is to have a clear picture of where you're standing now compared to everyone else. Like a GPS directional device, our Brand Positioning Assessment shows you where you are compared to the other experts in your field or similar fields.

It measures four key attributes of your brand:

// Brand Differentiation

How effectively does your brand capture the attention your audience?

// Brand Promise

How consistently does your brand deliver on its promises?

// Brand Relevance

How aligned is your brand to your audience and prospects' needs? The results of these two brand attributes determine your overall **Brand Distinction.**

// Brand Intelligence

How well do you understand your brand and the quality and impact of the brand experience on your audience? The results of these two attributes determine your **Brand Equity.**

A well-known and respected brand adds additional value (equity) to a thought leader's audience and will attract and positively influence new followers. That's why many market researchers agree that brand equity is one of the most important assets a thought leader can own.

BRAND POSITIONING ASSESSMENT

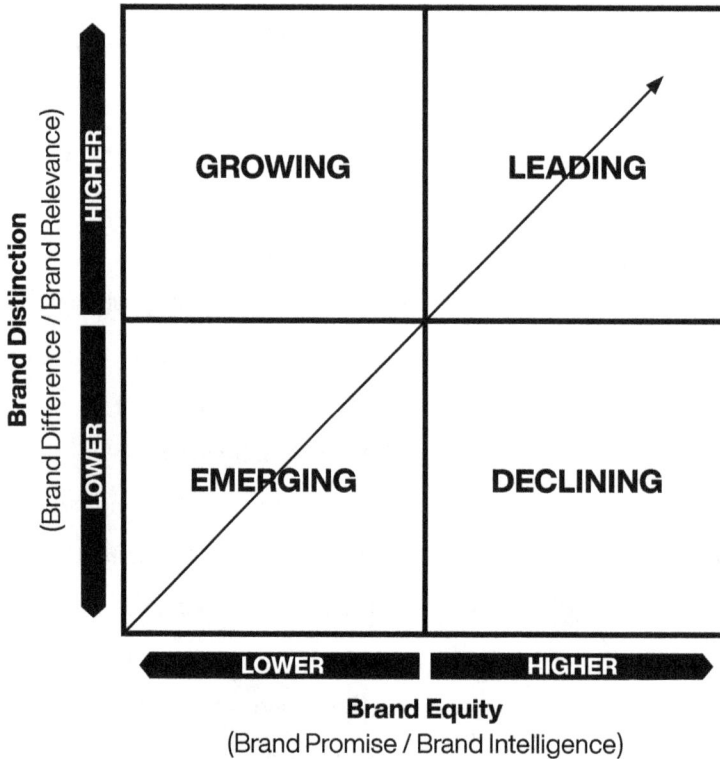

Brand Distinction
(Brand Difference / Brand Relevance)

HIGHER

LOWER

GROWING

LEADING

EMERGING

DECLINING

LOWER

HIGHER

Brand Equity
(Brand Promise / Brand Intelligence)

BRAND POSITIONING ASSESSMENT: Rate each of the four (Brand Distinction, Brand Relevance, Brand Promise and Brand Intelligence) on a scale of 1-10 (5 being the mid-level between lower and higher.)

INTRODUCTION IN BRIEF:

// A brand is more than a logo. It's a combination of visual and written elements that defines and identifies who you are, your values and beliefs, your reputation and your distinct advantage.

// A brand is an external reflection of the internal you and is possibly the most important asset you own as a thought leader.

// Your brand needs to be a conscious and deliberate creation that is positioned and aligned with who you are and what you stand for.

// Your brand needs regular scheduled time and resources allocated to maintain its different visual aspects and build on its equity.

TAKE ACTION:

☐ Describe your personal brand in 25 words or less.
☐ List three things that make you and your brand distinctive in your field.
☐ List one thing you feel you can do today to clarify your brand's most distinctive quality.

When you started in your field of expertise, maybe you had a picture of what you wanted to accomplish—a plan or goal that you hoped to achieve. there was something in that original plan that went beyond just standing out. **YOU WANTED TO "MAKE A DIFFERENCE."**

Then as your opportunities grew, the picture you envisioned has become less clear, overshadowed by the day-to-day details and demands of your daily tasks. You are working hard. You know you have the potential to be a better role model and leader, to work smarter and accomplish more, but you're just not sure how. You recognize that you're stalled, stretched to your limits, no longer certain of the direction in which your life is moving, or if you're making the right decisions. On some level, things just feel out of sync.

Be grateful. Within this moment of confusion, doubt and discomfort are the seeds of opportunity and breakthrough.

PURPOSE: WHAT YOU STAND FOR

When someone asks, "what do you stand for," how do you answer? Do you fumble for words, not quite sure what to say, or are you clear on the reason(s) why you do what you do in the world?

"What you stand for" is complicated—and it's also simple. It's a combination of things: values and principles that guide you; things you believe in; what you feel in your heart to be true; things that you love and are willing to make sacrifices for. It's all of these and more.

Think of it this way, what you stand for is like an inner compass. It points the way to your heart's truest and highest desire because the things you enjoy doing most will ultimately guide you to your greatest achievements and happiness.

How can you discover what you stand for? We can point you in the right direction and give you steps that will help lead you to your own truth. We can say that it takes self-reflection and examination of the qualities and values that make you who you are. We can say that what you stand for is more a matter of the heart than the head. But only you will answer this question for yourself.

Why? Because what you stand for—your purpose—is unique to you. Of all the billions of people in the world, you are an individual, born with a purpose and a reason for being that only you can know and feel with certainty. It's a gift that your talents, skills and courage will shape into something valuable that the world needs. So how do you start? And where do you look? Let me share a story that might shed some light on these question.

My sister Lorrie and I were born identical twins. We were lucky. We live in a world that expects differences in appearance and behavior. So, when people encounter two identical individuals (like Lorrie and I), they stop for a moment because identical twins challenge their assumptions about what they're seeing and the way they believe the world works.

Of course, identical twins are never exactly alike and some differ in profound ways. Yet, most people can't help but compare us, to figure out what's different so they can tell us apart. By taking a closer look at twins, we all can learn a great deal about the concept of differentiation and how individuals (like you) can find what they stand for and how best to stand out. I may look the same as my twin, but I always knew that I was different inside. So, from an early age, I was driven to find what made me different.

What my sister and I have learned over time is that it's our inner values, beliefs, talents, attitudes, and experiences that define who we are. These qualities are the foundation for discovering what we stand for and identifying our individual purpose. Our personal search for purpose has led us to where we are now—sharing what we've learned to help others.

// WARREN BUFFET

Warren Buffet is considered one of the most successful investors in the world. He stands out as a thought leader for sticking to the principle of "value investing," and being frugal with his personal finances. He has condemned the extravagant purchases by other CEOs and has a history of using public transportation.

Warren Buffet's Stand Out Statement:

Deliver the right parts exactly on time, exceed our internal and external customer requirements through continuous improvement, and provide a place for hard-working, dedicated, knowledgeable and ethical people who believe in the company.

WHAT DO YOU STAND FOR?

Now, more than ever, the world needs your individuality. All areas of society and business need your original thoughts, solutions and leadership. The world needs you to clearly define and communicate who you are—your inner values, beliefs, talents, attitudes and experiences. The world needs your passion and purpose to help shape the future and influence others.

What do you stand for? Whether you work alone or within a group or organization, whether your field of expertise is well established or still new, until you know what you stand for and learn to communicate that openly and honestly, the world won't know who you are or how you're different from anyone else.

What is it that makes you stand out? What makes you different from every other potential leader in your chosen field? You may think that you have innovative ideas, original solutions, a successful plan and a solid reputation. Guess what? So do a lot of others. To discover what makes you stand out, you must dig deeper into who you are and what you offer, because that's where your real differences live.

Why does it matter? While it may be worthwhile to note that you have important qualities and ideas that some consider valuable in your field, these qualities, in themselves, are not enough to distinguish you from the crowd.

In today's overcrowded mediasphere, your ability to stand out successfully is determined by your clarity about: 1. your purpose, 2. what you stand for, and 3. how you communicate it to the world. Knowing your purpose and what you stand for is a competitive advantage, but you also must let others know.

You must communicate and share your thoughts, ideas, and solutions. Only then can you be seen, recognized, and build trust about what you have to offer. With honest communication, you can stand out as an individual and a thought leader.

So, step out from the crowd. Stand for something you believe in and share it with others. When you're clear on what you stand for and live a life with purpose, you are unstoppable. When you know what you stand for, you can stand out—as a person, as a friend, and as a leader.

The world desperately needs better leaders, managers, partners, thinkers and doers—individuals who are authentic, true to what they stand for, and brave enough to stand up, stand out, and share their ideas to help answer the challenges the world faces today.

Courage—it's an essential ingredient in standing out. Stepping on stage, sharing your ideas and solutions can be scary. It takes courage or something else that comes from the heart. Let me share a story that shines a light on fear and courage.

Growing up, my dad was frequently my greatest teacher. He had a saying for everything and one my favorites was that "fear is the absence of love and love is the absence of fear."

When we pursue our purpose and know what we stand for, we lose our fear. For me, my *fear* comes from *not* working towards my purpose. *My courage* comes from helping others discover the difference they make in the world. Like the Cowardly Lion in the Wizard of Oz, when he was helping his friends, he naturally overcame his fears.

Here's a quick exercise about fear. Think of a time you were afraid of something (write that down). Where were you? Who was there? Where did you feel the fear? In your mind, your heart, or your entire being? How did you overcome that fear? And what did you learn from that experience? Now, think of a time and a situation when you were unafraid to do something (write that down). What felt different about the time you were unafraid and the time you were afraid? Did you feel more courageous when you were unafraid to face a situation? Or did you simply lose your fear when you committed to helping others?

Unless our fear is the result of an obvious physical danger, it can be something that our mind creates based on an uncomfortable experience we had in the past. Our mind remembers that and is reluctant to have that experience again. We spend a lot of time listening to our mind. And it's not always the best decision-making part of who we are. It's our hearts that have all the best answers.

Our challenge is that our brains are designed to make binary decisions—fight or flight—to avoid perceived life and death dangers and not become some dinosaur's snack. But in modern life there are many choices and options that don't match how our brains process and differentiate between whether a situation you face is life threatening or an opportunity for growth—like the decision to stand up, stand out and be recognized for the potential great thought leader you are.

Sometimes our fear is a sign of the exact thing we should do. And, instead of running away, we should be running towards it. Because in the process of moving towards that fear, we often find that we are no longer afraid. Instead, we feel energized. That's what courage feels like. So, if standing out and being recognized as a thought leader is scary, it may just be because it's exactly what you truly want and need to do.

// TONY ROBBINS Tony Robbins has empowered more than

50 million people from around the world through his educational programs, books, videos and live seminars. He is recognized by numerous publications as one of the world's most important leaders in personal development and business strategy.

Tony Robbin's Stand Out Statement:

I help others grow. We only feel fulfilled when we're improving ourselves or our lives in some way.

According to thought leader Tony Robbins, "The questions: 'What is my purpose in life?' and 'How can I be happy' are actually the same—and they have the same answer." When you discover what brings you joy, you usually reveal where your passions and your purpose live.

Now look at the illustration below to see how your purpose connects with and supports the driving force behind what you do.

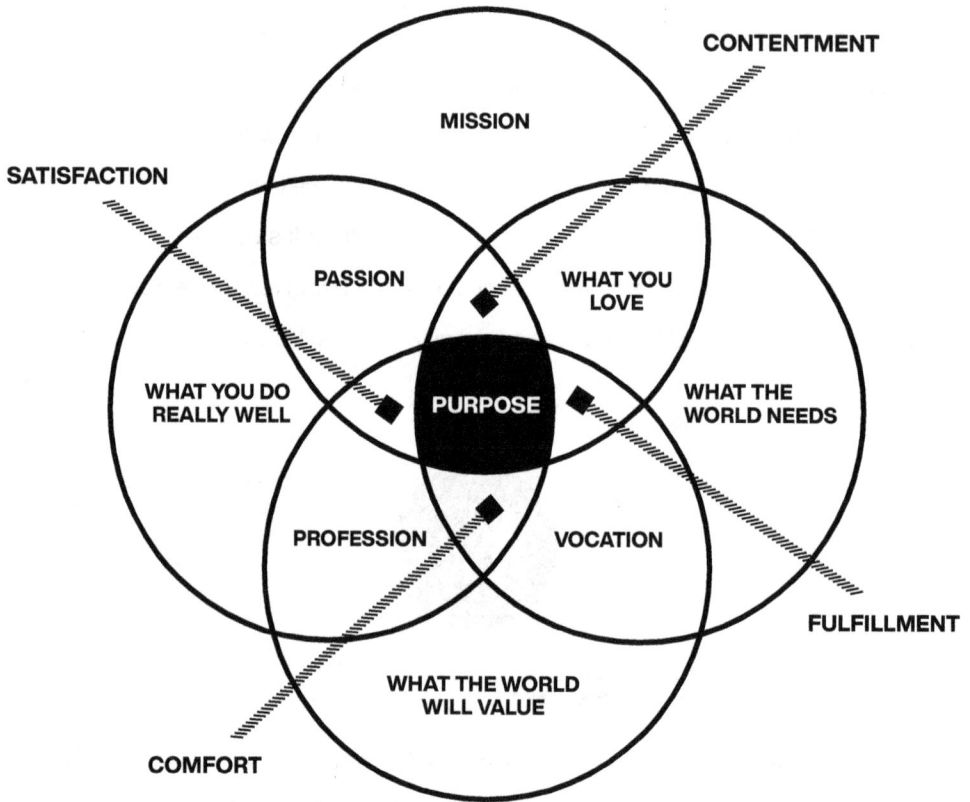

DISCOVERING YOUR PURPOSE

Are you unsure of your purpose? Possibly you never thought about it in these terms before but have a general concept of what *purpose* means.

PURPOSE EXERCISE: Make a list of the answers you provided to the questions below—these will help you discover different aspects of your purpose.

// WHAT DO YOU LOVE? WHAT ACTIVITIES DO YOU MOST ENJOY?

// WHAT DOES THE WORLD NEED?
WHAT DO YOU DO THAT ADDS VALUE TO THE WORLD?

// WHAT DO YOU DO REALLY WELL? WHAT ARE YOUR TALENTS AND SKILLS?
WHAT ARE THE THINGS YOU DO THAT HARDLY SEEM LIKE WORK?

// HOW COULD THE WORLD BENEFIT? WHAT DO YOU DO THAT OTHERS
VALUE AND NEED, AND HOW MIGHT IT MAKE OTHERS' LIVES BETTER?

"THE TWO MOST
IMPORTANT DAYS
IN YOUR LIFE ARE
THE DAY YOU
WERE BORN
AND THE DAY YOU
FOUND OUT WHY."
— MARK TWAIN

PURPOSE IS A VERB

Imagine that your purpose is a *verb* instead of a noun. Standing for something is great but acting with purpose and sharing your views can turn a good leader into a great leader and support change in your chosen field and the world.

Make your words and actions an authentic reflection of who you are and what you believe, and you'll naturally find your groove, hit your stride, and achieve maximum efficiency and impact. When you are being true to yourself, true to your values and beliefs, and true to your purpose, you can harness your full potential.

To become a thought leader, share your thoughts, views and opinions about your chosen field—in writing, through publishing in print or online, and through speaking and consulting. Start small, gain practice, and grow your audience.

By speaking and writing about your area of expertise and what you're doing that's different or distinct, you'll become even more familiar with your own uniqueness, and you may even inspire others to be more of who they are. Pay attention to how others react and respond to your message as well. You may get important new ideas for further growth and development from the comments and questions you receive.

// RICHARD BRANSON

Richard Branson is a thought leader because he broke the mold of the typical entrepreneur. Instead of being a tough and ruthless businessperson, he treats both employees and customers with kindness and respect. He breaks the rules, takes risks, genuinely cares about people, and doesn't give up.

Richard Branson's Stand Out Statement:

Treat people well and they will come back for more.

BENEFITS OF LIVING AND ACTING FROM YOUR PURPOSE

Living and acting with a clear purpose simply makes life work better. Remember, your purpose is your internal compass—you can refer to it as often as needed to ensure that you're "on purpose" with your actions and that your decisions are aligned with your deepest values and beliefs.

Acting with a clear purpose keeps you focused on delivering value and promotes positive relationships. Integrating your purpose into the way you communicate and act in the world can help you to stand out as an individual and take off as a thought leader.

PURPOSE ADDS SIGNIFICANT VALUE TO WHATEVER YOU DO

The value that you create by living and acting with purpose can't be measured only in terms of short-term profit or personal recognition. Look at how it sustains your immediate environment and creates conditions that allow for your purpose to unfold and develop over time.

Yes, that's right, your purpose evolves. Like traveling a winding mountain road, at times you can see clearly where your purpose is leading. Then the road turns and the path ahead is blocked from view. At those times, you'll learn to trust that your purpose is true. Know that each time you make another turn in the road, your purpose may become a bit clearer.

The remarkable thing about purpose is that when you follow it, when you let yourself be guided by that inner compass, you may come to see how your individual purpose is part of a much larger universal purpose.

Here are a few ways in which purpose adds value:

// Connects you to others: People learn to trust and follow a leader who is interested in the quality of their lives and proves it through words and actions.

// Builds relationships: Knowing and sharing your purpose helps people relate to you emotionally. In any relationship, truthfully sharing who you are encourages understanding, compassion and trust.

// Makes lasting impressions: Sharing your purpose creates rich ground for relationships to take root, grow and flourish. People may forget your last presentation or online post, but they don't forget a trusted relationship.

// Gets you noticed and remembered: People notice leaders when they're not just offering another commodity, but a solution or insight into something that will make a positive difference in the quality of other's lives.

// Provides focus: Knowing your purpose and implementing it into words and action allows you to focus on what really matters to stand out, grow and make a difference.

// Energizes you and your actions: Your goals and mission become clearer, more engaging and energizing when there's an expressed purpose behind what you do. Purpose helps attract people who will share your ideas and solutions with others.

// Fuels growth: Purpose empowers your decisions, shapes personal growth and supports honest and meaningful communications. It attracts others who align with your values and beliefs and who will support growth and change in your field of expertise.

WHAT YOU STAND FOR SHAPES THE IMPACT YOU HAVE ON THE WORLD

Identifying the characteristics that distinguish a true leader from his or her peers has never been more essential than today. Online reach and global media have drawn every thought leader into international focus. With these changes come expanded opportunities and also expanded exposure. If a leader does not tell his or her own story, someone else may very well tell one about them.

The question has become not only how can you stand out, but *what will you stand for*? It's crucial that you direct how you communicate and distinguish yourself in your field.

Standing out is a function of several things:

// Understanding and promoting your purpose and what guides you to do whatever you do

// Identifying your authentic self through personal and revealing stories, and then making this part of your communications

// Managing and promoting your reputation and your message within the mediascape and using the tools of today's communication media

Standing out is not a guarantee that you'll achieve your goals, but unless you step up and stand out, your ideas or solutions, no matter how creative or innovative, may never reach a world that needs desperately what you have to offer.

"EFFORTS AND COURAGE ARE NOT ENOUGH WITHOUT PURPOSE AND DIRECTION."
— JOHN F. KENNEDY

WHAT YOU WOULD DO IF...

PURPOSE "WHAT IF" EXERCISE: What if? What would you do if money were not an issue? The goal is to discover what you are passionate about and look for ways to bring that passion into realizing your purpose.

// **MONEY WERE NOT AN ISSUE:**

// **YOU COULD PURSUE YOUR FAVORITE THING TO DO:**

// **YOU COULD EXPLORE YOUR INTERESTS:**

// **YOU COULD START OVER:**

BIG SKY IDEAS: DIAMONDS ARE A BRAND'S BEST FRIEND

DIAMOND MINING EXERCISE: Look for opportunities to improve the way you communicate your ideas. Poll (your closest friends; your associates; your followers) and ask these questions: Where are the diamonds in my own back yard? What is the next idea or solution that is going to take me to the next level? What big sky idea is going to help me to stand out?

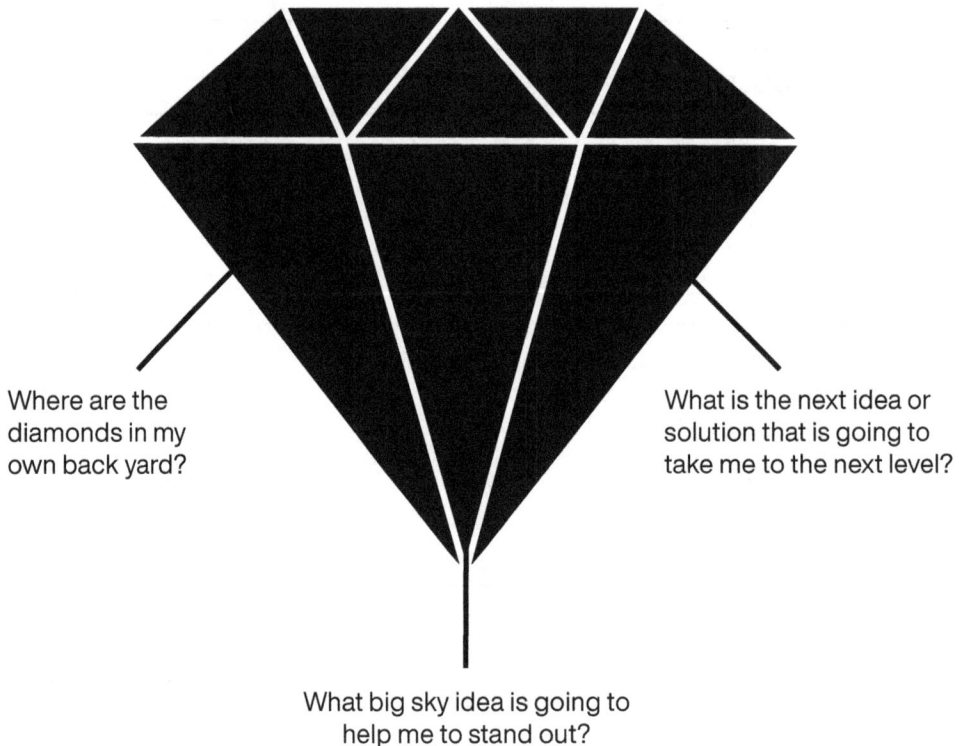

Where are the diamonds in my own back yard?

What is the next idea or solution that is going to take me to the next level?

What big sky idea is going to help me to stand out?

PURPOSE IN BRIEF:

// Your purpose is a combination of many things including personal values and principles, your heart's desire, and what brings you the greatest joy, but most of all it's why you do what you do in the world.

// Purpose is completely personal to you.

// Knowing your purpose and what you stand for is your first step in understanding how to stand out from the crowd.

// Standing for something you believe in and living a life with purpose has many benefits—and can make you unstoppable.

// Living a life with purpose adds value to whatever you do and makes your life work better.

// Overcoming the fear of standing out is a necessary step in a leader's personal growth.

// Your purpose evolves as you grow.

TAKE ACTION:

☐ Do one thing that brings you closer to what you would most love to do.
☐ Spend 15 minutes on something that will give you joy.
☐ In one sentence describe your purpose—why you do what you do.
☐ Describe in 25 words or less how what you do is utilizing your personal gifts and how that serves the world.

PROTECTING YOUR
REPUTATION IN TODAY'S
SOCIAL MEDIA WORLD HAS
BECOME A CHALLENGE.
IT'S HARD TO KNOW
**WHAT'S TRUE AND
WHAT ISN'T.**

MONITORING YOUR BRAND
PERCEPTION, INDUSTRY TRENDS
AND THE GLOBAL MEDIASPHERE.

REPUTATION

// IDENTIFY WHERE YOU STAND.

Which of these statements most accurately reflects your current
level of reputation monitoring and awareness?

- ☐ My reputation is not clear.
- ☐ My reputation is somewhat clear.
- ☐ My reputation is clear, but I do not monitor it; nor do I monitor
  my peers.
- ☐ My reputation is clear; I monitor my reputation but not that of
  my peers.
- ☐ My reputation is clear; I monitor my reputation regularly and
  consistently monitor my peers.

IN A SENSE, YOUR REPUTATION IS YOUR CURRENCY. Leaders with strong positive reputations are perceived as delivering more value through their ideas and solutions. **THEIR AUDIENCE IS MORE LOYAL AND FOLLOWS THEIR COMMUNICATIONS MORE REGULARLY.** This makes you especially vulnerable to anything that damages your reputation.

THE POWER OF KNOWING

When we were little, our dad used to say, "You don't know what you don't know." It was constant. He would drop us off at school, roll down the window and holler, "Winnie and Lorrie—remember, you don't know what you don't know." We would bow our heads quietly and keep going. Birthdays, friends over, Sunday dinners, he would say, "You don't know what you don't know." We would look at him and say "yeah dad…"

It took us a long time to "get it"—to understand what he was trying to teach us—to understand why he kept repeating himself and how it became a core way of thinking in our upbringing.

Fast forward to today—there is so much out there that we don't know. Do you know what people are saying about you right now? Do you know the condition of your personal reputation?

If not, then you need to get a clearer picture of these external perceptions because not knowing what your audience, connections, followers and promoters are saying can be detrimental to your role as a leader. Once upon a time, you didn't have to worry about what audiences or critics had to say about you. Opinions were shared within a small circle of people who leaders interacted with. A leader's reputation was more often shaped by the opinions expressed in the "press," by reporters and journalists, whose opinions were most often read locally by others.

Today, communication is a wide-open book where anyone can share their thoughts, opinions, compliments, complaints, and criticism about you online, anytime and anywhere. And the whole world can read what they write. Today, a negative opinion about you can be spread globally within moments and remain there available for others to read for years. So, how do you protect your reputation in this kind of environment?

SOMEONE IS TALKING ABOUT YOU RIGHT NOW. WHAT ARE THEY SAYING?

// Monitor religiously—Track what is being said about you, both the positive and negative comments, across all media as if your reputation depends on it. Because it does. Make consistent monitoring of your reputation your mantra—because negative perceptions and comments can, overnight, damage a reputation that you've built through years of hard work. And by monitoring, you can better plan your responses.

// Communicate, communicate, communicate—Honest and sincere communication is key to any healthy relationship and communicating with your connections is no different.

// Respond—Stay aware of your connections' and critics' perceptions and comments so you can respond to both positive and negative feedback in a timely manner. A slow response can communicate indecisiveness or worse, apathy. A timely response can help you avoid or limit possible damage to your reputation.

// Build goodwill—By being proactive and building goodwill through ongoing positive actions and comments, a thought leader can stay "ahead of the curve" and build a positive reputation that can minimize the potential damage of negative comments or criticism and lead to increased followers and promoters.

RELATIONSHIPS ARE BUILT ON TRUST

We've often said that business is built on relationships. And relationships, especially the relationships between thought leaders and their followers, are built on trust. It's not only the foundation of strong relationships, but a source of your distinct advantage and an essential strategy for standing out. In fact, Forbes magazine states that trust is "the most valuable commodity in today's business world."

// VINCE LOMBARDI As head coach and general manager of the Green Bay Packers, Vince Lombardi led his team to three NFL championships and two Super Bowl victories. As coach, general manager and part owner of the Washington Redskins, he led that team to its first winning season in 14 years. He became a national symbol and thought leader for single-minded determination to win.

Vince Lombardi's Stand Out Statement:

I help others discover the strength of their own will. The difference between a successful person and others is not a lack of strength, not a lack of knowledge, but rather a lack of will.

WHAT VALUE DO YOU DELIVER?

Your value proposition—is a summary of the benefits your ideas or solutions offer for your audience (what's in it for them), why they should believe you, and why your ideas are better than the status quo or other competing ideas or solutions. According to a MECLABS research study, an effective value proposition has four main components:

// Clarity — What exactly are you offering?

// Credibility — Can your audience trust what you offer?

// Appeal — How much does your audience desire what you offer?

// Exclusivity — Where else can they get what you offer?

VALUE PROPOSITION EXERCISE: Poll your audience. Ask what they believe is your primary value proposition (why they follow you). Collect the feedback and choose the value proposition most often mentioned as your number one. List the next five most frequent mentions as your secondary value propositions.

// WHAT IS YOUR PRIMARY VALUE PROPOSITION?

// WHAT ARE YOUR SECONDARY VALUE PROPOSITIONS?

ASK YOUR FOLLOWERS

One of the best ways to understand how you are perceived is to talk with your followers—ask for feedback from whoever makes up the audience for your ideas or solutions. And don't just talk at them—communicate with them.

Begin a two-way dialogue in which you listen to what your audience has to say about their response to your ideas and if what you're presenting fills their needs and makes their lives easier.

Speak to your audience as if you were sitting with them, in person, instead of composing a press release or reading a questionnaire. Be genuine when talking and express your interest in their opinions.

Then listen...

Listen openly to what they have to say instead of missing their words while mentally preparing a response. Giving your full attention to your audience members will make a lasting impression and give you new insights into what they truly think and feel about your ideas. And always take seriously what your followers tell you.

Let them know how valuable their opinion is by finding ways to act on their feedback and make improvements in the way you communicate. When you do, your ability to serve them in the future will be enhanced.

Say "thank you."

Show your audience you appreciate their time and their opinion by offering your thanks at the end of your conversation. Show gratitude for each person who follows you; express kindness and compassion for their attention and opinion and you'll attract more of the same.

Even if you have a marketing team, don't rely on someone else to communicate for you. Reach out and have a personal conversation with a person with a negative comment or criticism. It will keep you more connected with your audience as individual people and could change a critic into a follower or promoter.

Follow up and follow through. In your conversations with your audience, if you say you'll investigate something that you talk about, find an answer to a question they have, or that you'll do something about what caused them to have a negative experience, do it. **Your word is your contract.**

Following through on what you've said and then letting your audience know what was done will build trust, promote transparency and help cement your relationships. Manage your audience's expectations to ensure that you're not over-promising, and always follow through and communicate the results of your conversation. It will grow relationships and turn your conversations into opportunities for improvement.

// SIMON SINEK

Simon Sinek is recognized as a creative and business thought leader and unshakable optimist. From researching great leaders and organizations and how they think, act and communicate, he developed and popularized the concept of WHY—one's deepest reason for doing what they do in the world. He describes his "why" as: To inspire people to do the things that inspire them so that, together, each of us can change our world for the better.

Simon Sinek's Stand Out Statement:

I help others identify their purpose. People don't buy what you do; they buy why you do it. And what you do simply proves what you believe.

**"YOUR BRAND IS THE
SINGLE MOST IMPORTANT
INVESTMENT YOU CAN
MAKE IN YOUR BUSINESS."**
— STEVE FORBES

ARE YOU ACTIVELY MANAGING YOUR REPUTATION?

A large part of your value to your audience comes from hard-to-assess intangible things like "brand equity" and "intellectual capital." This makes a thought leader especially vulnerable to anything that damages his or her reputation.

Communications in all areas has changed dramatically in recent years. According to the Pew Research Center, roughly seven-in-ten U.S. adults say that despite a string of controversies and the public's relatively negative sentiments about aspects of social media, they still say they use some kind of social media site—a percentage that has remained relatively stable over the past five years. Respondents to the Pew Research Center survey (2021) said that YouTube is the most used online platform. Fully 81 percent of Americans say they use this video-sharing site, up from 73 percent in 2019.

Communication is a two-way process. Your audience can research and comment about you for any reason to a world-wide network of other potential followers (and critics). In this light, it's crucial that you regularly monitor what is being said about you and your ideas because there are multiple potential channels of conversation happening simultaneously around the world each day.

REPUTATION. Whether it reflects who we are or not, WE ALL HAVE ONE.

Without the knowledge of what is being said or written about you, you could be losing followers. Research has shown that many people trust online and word-of-mouth interactions or reviews more than traditional information sources, such as your website, printed materials or advertisements. If you are not monitoring every channel of communication, your reputation could be at risk before you even realize it.

RISKS OF A DAMAGED REPUTATION

Building a reputation from scratch can be easy when no one knows who you are. But once you are known and followed by an audience, a damaged reputation can be hard to rebuild. Your audience is more likely to remember and discuss a damaged reputation over something new and positive that you have said or accomplished, especially in the short term. There's a saying that time heals all wounds, but time alone may not mend a badly damaged reputation.

In a survey done by American Express, 60 percent of people said they always share their bad experiences and tell nearly three times more people about a bad experience than they do about a good one.

// SETH GODIN

Seth Godin is an entrepreneur, marketer, and business author and speaker. He is recognized as a thought leader in the areas of marketing and packaging for personal perspective on marketing and business. He and was inducted into the American Marketing Associations Hall of Fame in 2018.

Seth Godin's Stand Out Statement:

I help others discover their story. People do not buy goods and services, they buy relationships, stories and magic.

"IT TAKES 20 YEARS
TO BUILD A REPUTATION
AND FIVE MINUTES TO
RUIN IT. IF YOU THINK
ABOUT THAT, YOU'LL
DO THINGS DIFFERENTLY."
— WARREN BUFFET

A GOOD REPUTATION IS HARD TO BEAT. A BAD REPUTATION IS HARD TO OVERCOME.

If your reputation is damaged, these are steps you can take to begin rebuilding it if it's not beyond repair:

// Take Responsibility: The first step is to admit that something is wrong. If a critic writes about a supposed wrong that you've done, apologize to that individual or individuals in the same review. By doing this, the individual, and others, will see that you are serious about fixing your perceived mistake. This alone could start to reshape the person's opinion about you and whatever they perceive as negative about you or something you've said.

// Don't Ignore the Negative: Learn from negative reviews. After all, reputation is based on what people perceive to be true. Understanding the source of negative perceptions can assist you in repairing any potential damage and convert negative perceptions to positive ones.

// Continuous Monitoring: To maintain a positive reputation, you must monitor your online footprint frequently. This positions you as proactive in sustaining your reputation. Although bad reviews and negative press stories can seem terrible in the moment, a bad reputation can be turned around with genuine concern and conscientious and sincere effort.

KNOW WHEN TO STAND DOWN. THE ART OF OPEN LISTENING.

Every thought leader will experience times when it is more important to listen than to speak. Listening is essential to understanding how your message is being heard by your audience and followers.

It's not unusual for a passionate person to want to make sure to say all that they want and to be understood. But just as important as having your message understood is understanding how your message is being received by others. And the only way to gain that understanding is by listening and getting real-time feedback.

You might think listening is easy. All you need to do is stop talking and give the other person a chance to say what's on their mind. But true open listening, as we call it, takes focus, concentration and a willingness to be open to new information or feedback about your ideas.

Why is open listening difficult? According to Stephen Covey in The 7 Habits of Highly Effective People, our tendency is to do one of four things when another person responds to what we have said:

// **Evaluate:** We judge what someone is saying and agree or disagree.

// **Probe:** We ask questions from your own frame of reference.

// **Advise:** We give counsel, advice, or solutions to problems.

// **Interpret:** We analyze others' motives and behaviors based on our own experiences.

"If you're like most people," Covey writes, "you probably seek first to be understood. You want to get your point across. And in doing so, you may ignore the other person completely, pretend that you're listening, selectively hear only certain parts of the conversation, or focus on only the words being said, but miss the meaning entirely."

Another reason that open listening is hard for most of us is that our brains think several times faster than people speak, as much as four times faster, according to one source. That means while we're able to listen at 400 words per minute, the average person can only speak at about 100-150 words per minute. That leaves lots of time for our brains to be thinking of something else, to get impatient or be distracted.

The solution? Focus. Just listen and be open to whatever the other person says. Don't think about what you will say next or how you might respond to further emphasize your point. To quote Stephen Covey again, "Most people do not listen with the intent to understand; they listen with the intent to reply." When we truly listen openly, we can review and summarize the main points of the other's comments or question and then respond appropriately.

How do you make someone feel they've been heard? Make eye contact. Don't interrupt. When the person is finished, you can repeat back what you think they meant to make sure you understood what they said. If you're unsure of their meaning, ask a question like, "What I believe you're saying is this_____. Is that right?", or "When you say such and such, do you mean...?" Concise questions prove that you're listening and that you're taking in and considering what the other person said.

In his book *Power Listening: Mastering the Most Critical Business Skill of All*, author Bernard Ferrari says "good listening is the key to developing fresh insights and ideas that fuel your success." He says that while most people focus primarily on improving their ability to communicate and present their own views more effectively, they tend to overlook the importance of good listening and thereby miss important opportunities to learn and build trust and respect from their audience.

Research indicates that people who feel they're being listened to are more likely to engage with you in the future. Think about it. How do you feel when you know another person is listening to you?

Open listening also means watching. How someone responds to you can reveal almost as much as the meaning of their words. Does the person look nervous or agitated? Does the pitch of their voice seem high? What does their body language say? Do they seem relaxed, or tense and confrontational? Open listening can help you gather important non-verbal information and provide you with more meaning about what's being said.

Don't interrupt. Let the person speak without interrupting them. Let them say what they need to say. Often, they may just need to be listened to and heard. Let them have the spotlight for that moment and then use their comment as a way to show your ability to be an open and attentive listener.

Remember, you don't always have to respond immediately. A brief pause after a person's comment can allow you to consider what's been said, and in that moment, you have an opportunity to choose either to respond at that time or say that you will provide an answer or response after you've looked more deeply into the question or issue.

Follow-up. In an article for the Poynter Institute, Jill Geisler wrote that people like to feel they are heard and that their ideas matter. She says, "No matter how good a listener you are, you lose credibility if you fail to follow up on an issue raised in a conversation. Telling people when you will get back to them is a commitment worth making... and keeping."

Being a good listener is harder than most of us think. But learning and practicing open listening can have a positive impact on your future success as a thought leader and speaker.

REPUTATION SENTIMENT

Social media channels have created a new world for the expression of audience opinion. It is immediate and forever. **Do you know the quality of your online sentiment and engagement?**

REPUTATION SENTIMENT EXERCISE: Review your last 30 days of online mentions and separate those mentions by sentiment—positive, negative and neutral. Divide the pie into sections. (Ex. 3/4 positive, 1/4 negative and 1/4 neutral.) Set a goal to increase positive sentiment with specific actions.

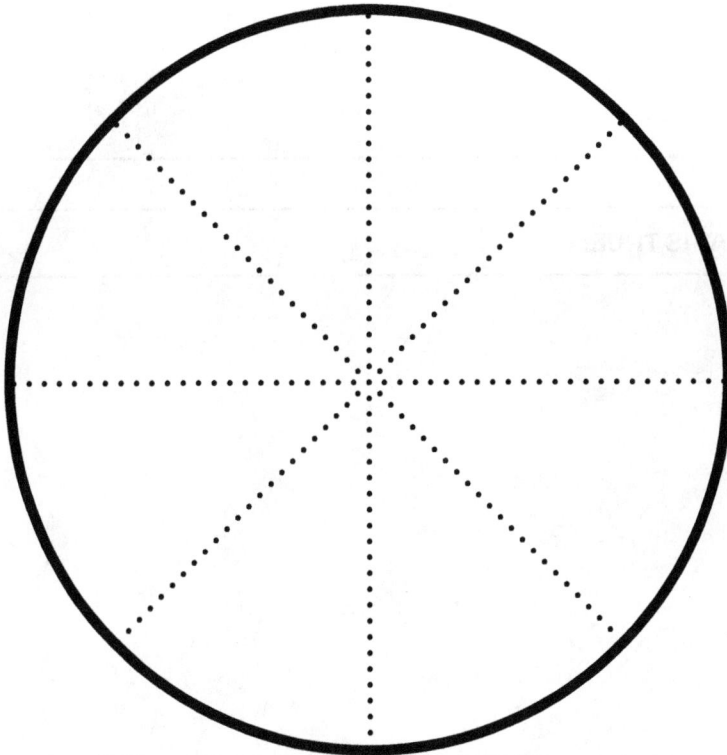

RUMOR SAYS

REPUTATION RUMOR EXERCISE: Consider key topics relative to your followers, brand, ideas or solutions. Look for ways to neutralize rumors and leverage truths.

// **WHAT I'VE HEARD RELATIVE TO MY BRAND:**

// **WHAT IS TRUE:**

REPUTATION IN BRIEF:

// Your reputation is invaluable—a strong positive reputation builds value and equity for your personal brand.

// There is power in knowing the condition of your reputation. Not knowing can be detrimental to your growth as a thought leader. How can you know? Ask your followers.

// Relationships are built on trust—trust is a source of your distinct advantage.

// You build trust through consistent and honest communications followed by action; your word is your contract.

// In today's world a leader's reputation must be managed and maintained regularly.

// A damaged reputation can be repaired with effort and through honest and genuine communication.

TAKE ACTION:

☐ In one or two sentences, describe your current reputation in your field.

☐ Let someone else who works in your field read it and get their feedback.

WE MAKE DECISIONS
ABOUT WHAT WE THINK
OF THOUGHT LEADERS IN
A MATTER OF SECONDS,
WITHOUT KNOWING VERY
MUCH ABOUT WHAT LIES
BELOW THE SURFACE.

THE OUTWARD APPEARANCE OF YOUR BRAND REFLECTS **WHO YOU ARE AND THE VALUE YOU DELIVER.**

IDENTITY

// IDENTIFY WHERE YOU STAND.

Which of these statements most accurately reflects how the perception of your brand reflects who you are and the value you deliver:

☐ The outward appearance of my brand does not reflect who I am or the value I deliver.

☐ The outward appearance of my brand somewhat reflects who I am and the value I deliver.

☐ The outward appearance of my brand is unique, reflects who I am and the value I deliver, but looks similar to other brands.

☐ The outward appearance of my brand is unique, reflects who I am and the value I deliver, but could use an upgrade.

☐ The outward appearance of my brand is a true reflection of who I am and reflects the value I deliver.

FIRST IMPRESSIONS. Growing up as a twin, you get used to the surprised double-take look you get when someone realizes for the first time that you're half of a set of twins. **FIRST IMPRESSIONS STICK WITH PEOPLE. WE ARE ALL AWARE OF THE POWER OF FIRST IMPRESSIONS.** That's why the way your brand looks is a crucial aspect of presenting the most accurate visual representation of your distinct advantage.

"IDENTITY" WE CALL IT. IT'S ONE OF THE MOST IMPORTANT FUNDAMENTALS— ONE THAT WE'VE BEEN STUDYING OUR ENTIRE LIVES.

Identity—is how can you present yourself through design in a way that honestly describes you and is a positive visual first-impression of how you wish to be known by others.

People like us trained in brand strategy love to talk about the visual aspects of branding because it's the fundamental that's closest to our hearts. However, good branding blends both strategic and creative perspectives. Like yin and yang, balance is what differentiates good design. Good design makes a powerful first impression and ensures you or your organization is noticed and remembered. **No small thing, Identity.**

TALK THE TALK.
WALK THE WALK.
LOOK THE PART.

Words, actions and visuals are the tools used to demonstrate the authenticity of the purpose of your brand. Consider "trading places" with your audience. The experience can give you the chance to discover and learn new insights. It allows you to view yourself through different eyes and experience your "identity" as others do.

A lot of people ask Lorrie and me if we've ever traded places. The answer is yes. In junior high school, we decided that the best time for us to try switching places was on Halloween. It was the first time that we thought we would be able get away with it. We went to school that day in costumes handmade by our grandmother, dressed as Raggedy Ann dolls. We thought it would take the matching costumes and makeup to be able to switch places. Sure enough, we exchanged classes that day and no one ever knew the difference.

We realize now that we didn't need the costumes and makeup to switch places, but that was the only time we intentionally tried it. However, today we're still trading places without actually doing anything. People often just assume we're the other twin!

In these situations, we don't say anything. We learn. It gives us a perspective about the life and relationships of the other twin. We get the chance to learn and gain insights into how each of us is seen by others.

This has also taught us how to "trade places" with others in our lives. While we can't swap identities with other people as easily as we can with each other, we take the time to imagine what it might be like to be our audience or our clients.

WHEN YOU ARE ABLE TO SEE YOURSELF OUTSIDE OF YOURSELF, YOU EXPERIENCE THE WORLD THROUGH AN ENTIRELY DIFFERENT LENS.

Here is a simple exercise that all thought leaders should attempt regularly. Look at your social media presence. Pretend that you are one of your own audience and search for yourself online. What comes up? What doesn't come up?

What does your website look like to someone who knows nothing about you or your message? What do your social channels look like? Would you respond to your own tweets and read the links that you post? Do you find your own content interesting? Compare your pages and channels to others and see the differences that your audience or your peers might notice right away. Try to view everything objectively.

Now imagine that you are one of your peers or competing thought leaders. Look at your online and offline presence from their point of view. Be as neutral as possible. Do you see any flaws or weaknesses? What are your peers doing better than you? What can you learn from them?

First impressions stick with people. Everyone in business is aware of the power of first impressions. That's why your brand's appearance is a crucial aspect of presenting the most accurate visual representation of what it is about you that is unique.

TWO-TENTHS OF
A SECOND

According to researchers at the Missouri University of Science and Technology, it takes less than two-tenths (.2) of a second for an online visitor to form a first opinion of you and your brand once they've browsed your blogsite or website. Following that, it takes just another 2.6 seconds for the viewer's eyes to track in a way that reinforces their first impression.

IT TAKES LESS THAN TWO-TENTHS OF A SECOND TO FORM AN OPINION.

Whew! Talk about pressure! But there are some indicators that will help you to work on the elements of your webpage or blogsite that are the most viewed in that first crucial second.

In that Missouri University study, the researchers employed eye-tracking software and an infrared camera to monitor participants' eye movements as they viewed the test website pages. Analysis of this eye movement showed how long people focused on specific portions of a web page before moving on to another part of the page.

In the next 1.23 seconds, the participants' eyes tracked seven elements on the web page, including the logo, navigation menus, search box, links to social utilities, the primary image, written content, and bottom of the page. They found participants spent about the same amount of time on each element. Participants were also asked to rate the test websites on their visual appeal and design. The same seven elements garnered the most interest and evaluation.

PEOPLE DO JUDGE A BOOK BY ITS COVER

The saying "don't judge a book by its cover" is a metaphorical phrase that means "you shouldn't prejudge the worth or value of something by its outward appearance alone." But the truth is, all too often, we do.

As twins, Lorrie and I have developed a heightened awareness of the importance of perception and reality. Being constantly mistaken for my sister and vice-versa can do that.

We share the distinct advantage of having a living mirror reflection of what we look like from outside ourselves. Like no one else, my sister can observe me and honestly say, "We look terrible in green." Or "I'm not sure if you realize that when you said such and such, it actually came across like something else." Or "Yes, your design may be out-of-the-box creative, but is it consistent with the client's brand, and how can we measure its success?"

From the firsthand experience of dealing with misperceptions and working hard to refine our individual identities, we've honed our ability to perceive distinct differences in other people, other companies and other brands. In our line of work, we use this ability to help our clients learn to see themselves and their brands more objectively.

Even though **FIRST IMPRESSIONS** are important, they're often based on very limited information that may include emotions, moods and prior memories or experiences.

"YOU NEVER GET A SECOND CHANCE TO MAKE A FIRST IMPRESSION."
— WILL ROGERS

BRAND REALITY CHECK IN THREE WORDS

What 3 words would you use to describe yourself? What if I asked someone who you had just met to describe you with just three words? And then, what if I asked someone who has known you for years to do the same? Three words that describe and capture who you are. Then compare those descriptions.

This can reveal the perception gap that we confront when creating and maintaining a personal brand—the difference between how you perceive yourself and how others perceive you. In each case, perception reflects a different reality of your brand. This exercise demonstrates the power of first impressions and the gap between how we wish to be perceived and how successful we are in communicating our brand reality to others.

// DEEPAK CHOPRA

Deepak Chopra, founder of the Chopra Foundation, is a recognized thought leader in Mind-Body health, integrative medicine, meditation and well-being, and alternative medicine.

Deepak Chopra's Stand Out Statement:

I work to offer alternative options for dealing with modern problems of health and well-being. The most creative act anyone can ever undertake is the act of creating oneself.

BRAND DESCRIPTION

BRAND DESCRIPTION EXERCISE: What four (4) words from the following list would you use to describe your brand?

	AGGRESSIVE		INTENSE
	AMBITIOUS		INNOVATIVE
	BOLD		INSPIRED
	BUSY		LOYAL
	CAPABLE		OPEN
	CARING		ORGANIZED
	COCKY		PASSIONATE
	COLD		PREDICTABLE
	CONSERVATIVE		RELIABLE
	CONFIDENT		REVOLUTIONARY
	CONFUSED		SINCERE
	CREATIVE		SMART
	DETERMINED		STRATEGIC
	EAGER		STRONG
	EFFECTIVE		SUCCESSFUL
	ENLIGHTENED		SUPERIOR
	ENTHUSIASTIC		SYSTEMATIC
	FORMAL		TALENTED
	GLAMOROUS		TRUSTWORTHY
	IMPRESSIVE		UNIQUE
	INFORMAL		VERSATILE

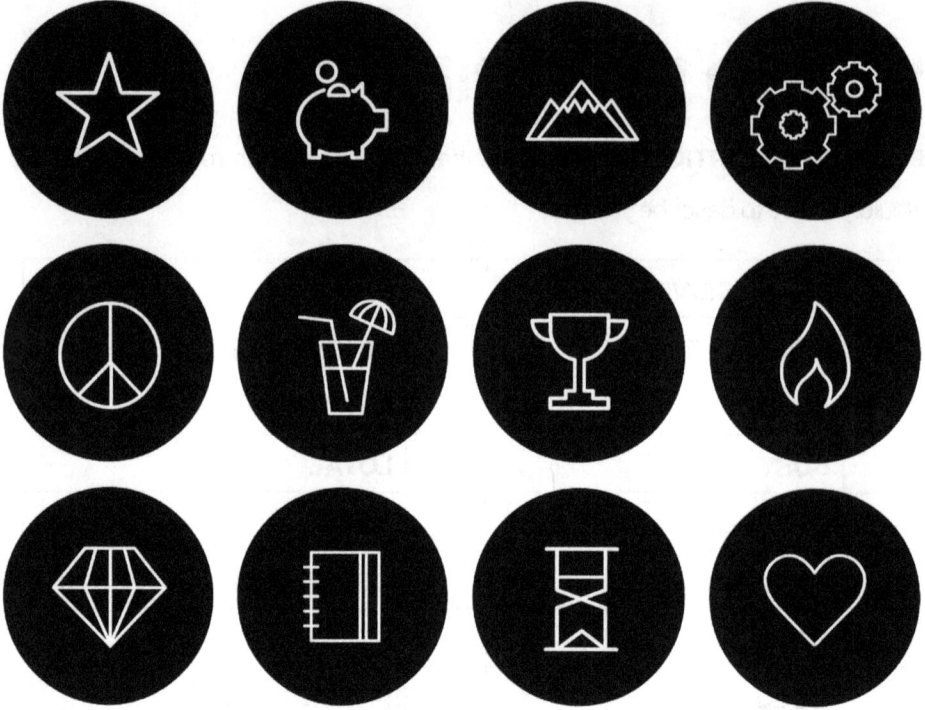

SYMBOLS HAVE MEANING.
WHICH OF THESE SYMBOLS WOULD YOU
ASSOCIATE WITH YOUR PERSONAL BRAND?

MY TOP SYMBOLS:

// SYMBOL:

// SYMBOL:

// SYMBOL:

IT'S ALL ABOUT THEM.

It's likely that the first impression a potential follower has of you will be a mix of words and images—a YouTube video, social media post, podcast, an ad or the results of an online search that turns up a blog post or news story.

Some potential thought leaders can be self-focused in their communications, marketing and promotion. After all, their ideas, solutions, seminars or workshops are what they are most familiar with and focused on. When they describe themselves or their ideas, their language may tend to be "I" or "we" statements, like "we do this;" or "I believe that." But the truth is this: your audience is far more interested in what your ideas or actions can do for *them*. Will it save them time or money? Will it make them happier or healthier? These are the things that will motivate them to respond to your message.

For your communications to be effective, you must learn to view your message from your audience's perspective—to see yourself from outside yourself. Replace the "I" and "we" in your communications with "you." Tomorrow, when you start your day, you can decide to change your mood and the direction of your life with one small thing—smile at everyone you meet. That one small thing can start a positive ripple that could make a difference in the lives of others in ways you can never imagine. Kindness is your best first impression. Kindness creates more kindness.

With every communication or interaction, ask yourself: How will this benefit the person in the audience who sees or hears this? How will this affect their experience of me and the ideas or concepts that I represent and promote? Will my audience feel what I say is valuable and will it fill *their* needs?

FACE VALUE

Professor of psychology at Princeton University, Alexander Todorov, was fascinated by the social psychology of faces during his years as an undergraduate student. He noted that previous research showed how even the glimpse of a face could create a strong impression on an observer based on the facial features. Studies had found that thin lips and wrinkles at the corners of someone's eyes communicated that a person was intelligent, distinguished or determined. Persons with baby-faces were judged as naïve and physically weak yet also honest and kind. Attractiveness was often equated with competence and masculinity with dominance. Not surprisingly, people also frequently said that they liked faces with features similar to their own.

Todorov conducted a major study at Princeton on the outcome of elections to learn if simple images of candidates that prompted "quick, unreflective judgments based solely on their facial appearances," would influence voting more than what a candidate said or believed, despite millions of dollars spent on their political information campaigns.

The people surveyed rated photographic images of previous congressional candidates for traits of competence. The results showed that "candidates perceived as 'more competent' turned out to have won 71.6% of the Senate races and 66.8% of the House races—far more than chance alone might allow. This single trait of competence projected by the candidate's photographic image influenced the outcome of political races more than all other traits combined."

PERCEPTION IS REALITY

The reality of your personal brand is a combination of your visual impression and your audiences' perception of the *authenticity* of that visual impression. Both are equally important. A person may take your word on first impression about who and what you say you are and the image that you project of yourself. Or, they may feel something is not quite right. Their longer-term experience of what you project and what you do will either confirm or change their first impression, favorably or unfavorably.

Expensive advertising can't compensate for a weak visual brand, unfounded ideas, and especially, a negative audience experience.

Leaders in the field of audience experience include these imperatives in developing their strategies:

// Design the appropriate key message for each segment of your audience.

// Define a positive "you-focused" message and keep it consistent with each of your audience segments.

// Deliver the highest quality audience experience consistently.

// Never stop trying to improve your audiences' experience; innovate.

// Own the issues. Be a part of the solution.

// Understand individual audience needs and work backwards to create an experience that exceeds expectations.

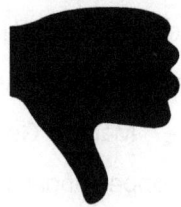

DOPPELGANGERS

A doppelganger is defined as a look-alike or double of a living person, sometimes portrayed as a paranormal phenomenon, and in some traditions and cultures as a harbinger of bad luck (the evil twin).

In advertising, the doppelganger has a couple of different meanings. One form of the phenomenon is ads or logos that are intentionally created to look like a familiar brand but altered by digital technology. A more insidious example is the creation of an actual ad campaign to look like and undermine the competition. Between 2006 and 2012, Apple ran the "I'm a Mac" campaign that contrasted the ease of use and speed of the Mac and PC computers in a humorous fashion. Not only did the campaign go viral, but it also helped grow sales for Apple by an estimated 39%.

Markus Geisler gives this definition in the AMA Journal of Marketing: "A doppelganger brand image is a family of disparaging images and stories about a brand that are circulated in popular culture by a loosely organized network of consumers, anti-brand activists, bloggers, and opinion leaders in the news and entertainment media." Underscore the word "disparaging" in this definition since most doppelgangers are negative, like substituting the term "Starsucks" for "Starbucks." Not only well-known brands are affected by this tactic and not all campaigns take the form of harmless puns. While some disparaging inferences may have no basis in fact, the most dangerous ones do.

Consider using this information about doppelgangers as a diagnostic tool to proactively manage the vulnerabilities of your branding efforts—how might your brand be copied, satirized or otherwise made fun of?

FEELING BLUE?

There has been much discussion and debate on the psychology of color in marketing. While many believe that color is too personal a matter to be universally applicable to trends, there are some research-backed insights that have merit and deserve consideration here in relation to a personal brand.

In the study *Impact of Color in Marketing*, researchers determined that people make up their minds within 90 seconds of their initial interaction with a product and that 62-90% of that assessment is based on color alone. Prudent use of color can contribute not only to differentiation but to attitudes towards a brand.

In the course of her studies into the *Dimensions of Brand Personality*, psychologist and Stanford University professor, Jennifer Aaker, concluded that there is a real connection between the use of colors and customers' perceptions of a brand's personality. Her findings indicate that certain colors broadly align with specific traits, i.e., brown with ruggedness, purple with sophistication, and red with excitement. In addition, and in agreement with other academic research, such as *The Interactive Effects of Color*, she suggests that a brand's colors should support the personality being portrayed rather than aligning with stereotypical color associations. In other words, colors must "fit" logically with the subject.

The bottom line is that there are no easy, clear-cut guidelines for choosing a brand's colors, but color is an essential consideration. Color helps create the feeling, mood and image that your brand communicates, and these elements play a subtle role in the message of who you are, or what you stand for.

When creating a new brand, it's important to use colors that ensure differentiation from well-known and established peers. What color best represents your personal brand?

WHAT IS YOUR TRUE PERSONALITY COLOR?

What color is your personality? Is it blue, green, red, yellow, black or white? It is this instinctual choice of a color that tells you a lot about yourself, how you function and how others see you. Your color choice reflects the way you operate in the world, your strengths and weaknesses. Your personality color does not have to be one you wear all the time but the one you are drawn to in what you wear; it is often your favorite, the color that excites you the most.

// ECKHART TOLLE

Eckhart Tolle is one of the most popular spiritual teachers and author in the world today. His books, videos and public appearances have introduced millions of people globally to the concept of joy and freedom available from living in the present moment. His bestselling books, *The Power of Now and A New Earth* have been translated into 52 languages.

Eckhart Tolle's Stand Out Statement:

I point out the importance of realizing deeply that the present moment is all you have. Make the NOW the primary focus of your life.

BLUE

trustworthy, dependable, strong, youthful, faith

If somebody says,
"you are loyal, committed and creative",
"you have a fixed set of principles",
"you get the job done even in stressful situations"
...blue may be your color.

// BLUE MAY BE MY COLOR:

GREEN

peaceful, healthy, calm, natural, friendly

If somebody says,
"you are a natural peacekeeper",
 "you strive for comfort",
"you need to love and be loved"
...green may be your color.

// GREEN MAY BE MY COLOR:

YELLOW

energy, fresh, happy, optimistic, confident, fun

If somebody says,
"you are persuasive",
"you are a natural-born salesperson",
"you are excellent at getting people aligned"
...yellow may be your color.

// YELLOW MAY BE MY COLOR:

RED

exciting, fiery, bold, love, aggressive, active, desire

If somebody says,
"you are dominant and powerful",
"you look at tasks without emotion",
"you make difficult decisions with ease"
...red may be your color.

// RED MAY BE MY COLOR:

BLACK

balanced, confident, luxurious, sensible, formal

If somebody says,
"you are independent",
"you are strong-willed",
 "you are decisive and confident"
...black may be your color.

// BLACK MAY BE MY COLOR:

WHITE

calm, peaceful, humble, classy, consistent

If somebody says,
"you avoid confrontation and are incredibly patient",
"you work well in groups",
"you get along with everyone, even difficult people"
...white may be your color.

// WHITE MAY BE MY COLOR:

"THE MOST POWERFUL BRANDS ARE BUILT FROM THE HEART. THEIR FOUNDATIONS ARE STRONGER BECAUSE THEY ARE BUILT WITH THE STRENGTH OF THE HUMAN SPIRIT, NOT AN AD CAMPAIGN."
— HOWARD SCHULTZ

COMMUNICATION DESIGN

The AIGA (American Institute of Graphic Artists) states that graphic design, also known as communication design, is the art and practice of planning and projecting ideas and experiences with visual and textual content. The form of the communication can be physical or virtual and may include images, words or graphic forms. The experience with communication design can take place in an instant or over a long period of time.

The scope of communication design can be at any scale, from the design of a single postage stamp to a national postal signage system, or from a thought leader's digital avatar (an icon or figure that represents your image) to the sprawling and interlinked digital and physical content of an international newspaper or magazine. Communication design can also be used for any purpose, whether commercial, educational, cultural or political.

My early background and training were in communication design. I was educated in a pre-digital classic design curriculum, and I learned the art and trade of traditional graphic design. I also served as President of the Art Directors and Designers Association. What I learned *then* is vastly different from what I do *now*—with two exceptions: the art of communication design is the same, though more sophisticated today, and the challenges have become even greater with how to build communication forms and channels, across a wider variety of media, that fulfill a specific purpose and provide a unique and positive experience.

If your goal is differentiation and how to stand out as a thought leader, good design should focus on clarifying and simplifying ideas, not on dressing them up. When you look around, you may find other thought leaders who have embraced effective communication design. You'll see that what they say and how they look accurately represent the truth of who they are and the authenticity of their message. The complete "design" (including message and identity) creatively simplifies and supports what they communicate to their audience.

Design differentiates. It distinguishes the look and feel of a thought leader and his or her ideas or solutions as well as the values and personality behind it. Design can reflect a leader's personality and thinking, and in today's world, audiences choose leaders, ideas, solutions, causes, movements and organizations that mirror their own values, personalities and lifestyles. Design influences individual decisions and is a source of competitive advantage that positively impacts a thought leader's credibility and growth.

Steve Jobs once said, "Design is not just what it looks like and feels like. Design is how it works." This doesn't imply that functionality is more or less important, but today when an audience has a choice between two similar ideas, the aesthetics of the design can be the deciding factor in the decision to follow one or the other thought leader.

As the communications environment evolves and society's issues change, the process of communication design will generate new and more effective ways to design ideas, messages and solutions. If we look at current trends as indicators, we can make a few assumptions: authenticity and truth are increasingly valued; ecologically oriented or "green" solutions are crucial as are ideas and solutions that deal with social issues. In all cases, more people desire new thinking and new creative directions and approaches to today's and tomorrow's challenges.

"Design is the method of putting form and content together. **DESIGN, HAS MULTIPLE DEFINITIONS**; there is no single definition. Design can be art. Design can be aesthetics. **DESIGN IS SO SIMPLE, THAT'S WHY IT'S SO COMPLICATED.**"
— Paul Rand

LOOK AT YOUR PERSONAL BRAND FROM EVERY PERSPECTIVE

Is it consistent? When you watch a video, read a social post, or view a website—is the message and experience the same?

// IS MY BRAND CONSISTENT?

"DESIGN IS NOT JUST WHAT IT LOOKS LIKE, DESIGN IS HOW IT WORKS"
— STEVE JOBS

BRAND CONSISTENCY

BRAND CONSISTENCY EXERCISE: **4.0+ Excellent; 3.5 good; 3.0 marginally okay; 2.5 needs much improvement; 2.0 badly hurting business. Ratings: 1=lowest; 5=highest.

	Consistency	Quality

Brand Visual Identity:

	Consistency	Quality
Logo	① ② ③ ④ ⑤	① ② ③ ④ ⑤
Website	① ② ③ ④ ⑤	① ② ③ ④ ⑤
Social Media Channels	① ② ③ ④ ⑤	① ② ③ ④ ⑤
Marketing Materials	① ② ③ ④ ⑤	① ② ③ ④ ⑤
Buildings/Workspace	① ② ③ ④ ⑤	① ② ③ ④ ⑤
Promotional Items	① ② ③ ④ ⑤	① ② ③ ④ ⑤
Advertising	① ② ③ ④ ⑤	① ② ③ ④ ⑤
Sales Collaterals	① ② ③ ④ ⑤	① ② ③ ④ ⑤
Video/Animation	① ② ③ ④ ⑤	① ② ③ ④ ⑤
Customer Experience	① ② ③ ④ ⑤	① ② ③ ④ ⑤
Personal Appearance	① ② ③ ④ ⑤	① ② ③ ④ ⑤
Other: _____	① ② ③ ④ ⑤	① ② ③ ④ ⑤
_____	① ② ③ ④ ⑤	① ② ③ ④ ⑤
_____	① ② ③ ④ ⑤	① ② ③ ④ ⑤
_____	① ② ③ ④ ⑤	① ② ③ ④ ⑤

Total Rating Points

Overall Evaluation**

BRAND PERCEPTION

BRAND PERCEPTION EXERCISE: Ask both questions. Identify the significant differences, and brainstorm ways to align them.

// HOW DOES THE WORLD PERCEIVE YOUR PERSONAL BRAND? (ACTUAL)

// HOW DO YOU WANT THE WORLD TO PERCEIVE YOUR PERSONAL BRAND? (IDEAL)

WHO DO YOU MOST ADMIRE?

WHO DO YOU MOST ADMIRE EXERCISE: Look at the thought leaders in your or other fields as well as influential (or inspirational) brands that you like. What about them (from a first impression approach) might appeal to an audience? What do you admire about them? What can you learn from them and/or bring to your brand strategy?

// INDUSTRY LEADERS

// BRAND INFLUENCERS

LOOKING THE PART

Being consistent with your brand also applies to how you look—your appearance. What you wear and how you look from outside of yourself to your followers is a significant part of your personal style and identity. You can learn to see yourself from outside of yourself by communicating with others that you trust. Though it helps to have an identical twin like my sister and me, it isn't essential to get accurate and reliable feedback on whether your outward appearance is an honest reflection of who you are and what you stand for.

Your public image and personal brand should always be an honest reflection of your beliefs, personal tastes, core values and authentic personality traits but you're positioning yourself as a leader in your industry. What would your audience think a leader in your field should look like? If you're unsure, ask your close friends or look at other leaders in your field. Looking the part is important to your credibility.

// HOW WOULD YOU DESCRIBE YOUR APPEARANCE?

WHAT DO YOU SEE?

RORSCHACH INKBLOT TEST: To introduce the concept that we all see things differently, share this Rorschach inkblot test. This is a psychological test in which subjects' perceptions of inkblots are analyzed using interpretation and complex algorithms.

// WHAT DO YOU SEE?

(Source: Rorschach test, Wikipedia)

IDENTITY IN BRIEF:

// The outward appearance of your brand (and you) communicates who you are and what value your ideas and solutions deliver.

// First impressions are lasting; people do judge a book by its cover.

// Your identity is the totality of the visual impression you make. You are your brand.

// Learning to "see yourself from outside yourself" is essential to creating and building a personal brand.

// With every communication or interaction, consider the impression you make from your audiences' perspective.

// The colors you use with your brand should logically and emotionally fit who you are and what you stand for.

// Consistency of your brand's visual elements and message are both essential for growth and building trust.

TAKE ACTION:

☐ Ask two people to give you their honest opinion of how you are perceived by your outward appearance.

☐ Ask someone who doesn't know you if they can guess what field you work in by your outward appearance.

ARE YOU HONEST AND TRANSPARENT WHEN YOU COMMUNICATE? ARE YOU CONSISTENT WITH YOUR **TRUE STORY?**

YOUR MESSAGE IS CONSISTENT, TRUE, GENUINE AND COMMUNICATES VALUE TO YOUR AUDIENCE AND FOLLOWERS.

AUTHENTICITY

// IDENTIFY WHERE YOU STAND.

Which of these statements most accurately reflects the current quality of your message?

- ☐ My message is not clear.
- ☐ My message is somewhat clear.
- ☐ My message is clear but not consistent.
- ☐ My message is clear, consistent, and genuine but it does not communicate my value propositions.
- ☐ My message is clear, consistent, and genuine and it communicates my value propositions.

WHEN WE DISCUSS AUTHENTICITY, WE FOCUS ON YOUR MESSAGE. That's because you express your authenticity through your words and prove it through your actions. When a leader's words match who they are and what they believe and their actions match their words, they are being authentic. **START WITH THE QUESTION: "WHO ARE YOU?" YOU ARE MADE UP OF LAYERS.** To be truly authentic, you must examine each of these layers until you reach the core of your beliefs, vision and goals. This is where you find who you are and what you represent as a thought leader. When you're making decisions as a thought leader (remember the internal compass idea?) every choice you make should reflect who you are. Your authentic self is a collection of all the things that make you and your story unique and individual—your passions, talents, inclinations, life experiences, and especially your values and beliefs.

YOUR STAND OUT STATEMENT

Your stand out statement is a short, one sentence statement that you want your audience and followers to hear, understand and remember. It describes you and the ideas or solutions you promote and how they logically connect with who you are and what you stand for. Your stand out statement provides clarity and focus about the "why" behind what you say and do.

People are likely to remember little of all the information you present at any given time or through any media—live, in-person, streaming online, or recorded. Your stand out statement is what you would say if you only had 5 seconds to say it. It's a short few words that capture the essence of your primary message.

It should include the specific words or ideas that you would use to build longer communications. The words you use and the emotional and logical appeal they include will be the building blocks for your elevator speech, your personal story and other communications you develop to express your ideas, solutions, or point of view.

Your stand out statement should be:

// Clear—relevant, lacking technical language, and memorable.

// Concise—One short sentence, that encapsulates who you are and what you stand for.

// Consistent—You should use this with every communication, repeatedly, if it is to sink in and be remembered.

HIERARCHY OF CONTENT. This funnel chart shows the various layers of types of messages you communicate and how they connect from large to small.

// **Content**—The material dealt with in a speech, presentation, book, website, or research paper

// **Topic**—The particular focus of your content

// **Key Messaging**—An outline of the main points of your content

// **Primary Message**—A one or two-sentence summary of your content

// **Stand Out Statement**—One sentence that describes how or why your idea of solution helps others

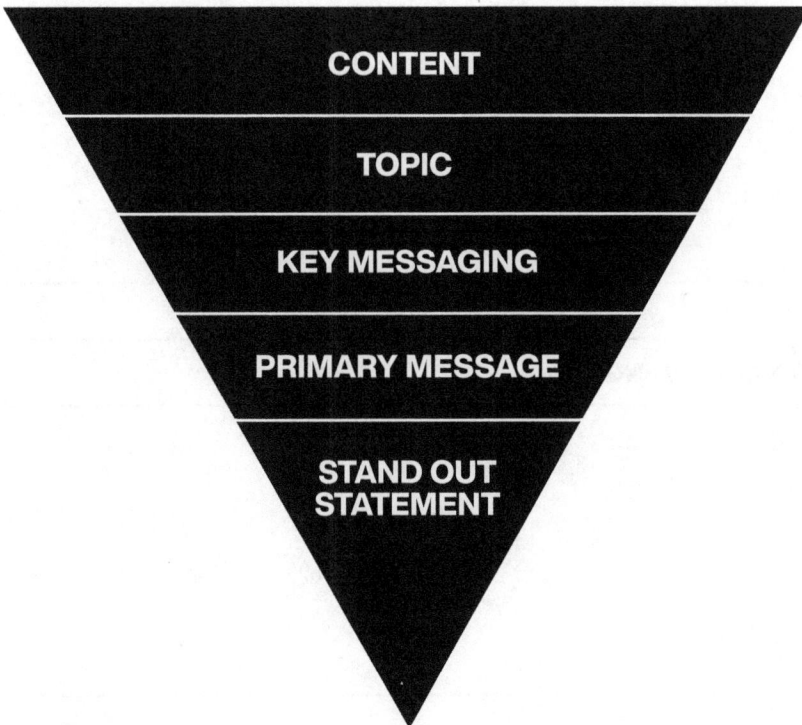

CONTENT

TOPIC

KEY MESSAGING

PRIMARY MESSAGE

STAND OUT
STATEMENT

STAND OUT STATEMENT:

// CONTENT:

// TOPIC:

// KEY MESSAGING:

STAND OUT STATEMENT:

// **PRIMARY MESSAGE:**

// **STAND OUT STATEMENT:**

Stand Out Statement Examples:

// I help potential leaders stand out because I believe the world will improve with better leaders.

// My ideas can reduce global warming and the negative effects of climate change.

// I am working to help improve communication, compromise and global cooperation.

// The technique I teach can help individuals reach their full potential.

"THERE'S A SIMPLE RULE: YOU SAY IT AGAIN, AND YOU SAY IT AGAIN, AND YOU SAY IT AGAIN AND AGAIN AND AGAIN, AND ABOUT THE TIME THAT YOU'RE SICK OF SAYING IT IS ABOUT THE TIME YOUR TARGET AUDIENCE HAS HEARD IT FOR THE FIRST TIME."

— FRANK LUNTZ

YOUR BRAND VOICE

Your brand voice is a combination of the tone of your communications, the particular words you choose, and the style of writing and sentence structure you use to express the information you communicate.

Your brand voice may also be described as your authentic voice. Regardless of your background or area of expertise, the more honest and authentic your story and the words you choose, the more your words will resonate and ring true with your audience. Simple and honest words delivered from the heart will have greater impact, and you'll feel better about what you say and the work you do.

Your brand voice should be distinctive and recognizable—like your individuality—and become an integral part of your brand identity. Consider for a moment the distinct differences in the language we use every day, in writing and in speaking, and note how these differ. In speaking, we use more colloquial, everyday words and expressions and more relaxed, less structured sentences. In writing, especially in formal business writing, communicators tend to use more structured sentences. They communicate complete thoughts and strive for clarity and simplicity to be better understood.

"Authenticity is a collection of choices that we have to make every day. **IT'S ABOUT THE CHOICE TO SHOW UP AND BE REAL.** The choice to be honest. The choice to let our true selves be seen."
— Brené Brown

YOUR BRAND VOICE IS AN EXTENSION OF YOUR PURPOSE.

Everything begins with your purpose in creating your personal brand, even your brand voice. That's because your brand voice expresses who and what you are—your values and your identity—in words.

Your brand voice, like your core values, allows you to connect authentically with your audience—to inform, engage, influence and persuade. You naturally choose words and ideas that your audience can understand and relate to.

Your brand voice combined with your visual identity (visuality) should be based on a coordinated strategy. They should work together to create a consistent and purposeful expression of who you are and the ideas or solutions you promote.

Brand voice and social media voice—the differences.

Your brand voice and social media voice both represent who you are as a thought leader, but they are different. These voices and the personality they reflect help bring your brand to life. Here are some points that help describe the differences:

Brand Voice:

// Accurately reflects your brand personality

// Is a single recognizable voice involved in one-way communications

// Is consistent across mediums

// Is unique to you

Social Media Voice:

// Involves a conversation between real people

// Reflects your brand as less formal and more personal

// Is a two-way dialogue that's informative and engaging

// Listens, learns and responds

ARCHETYPAL BRANDS

Want to make your brand story more powerful and memorable? Find out what qualities you have that are like those of well-known archetypes.

Archetypes are a concept developed by Swiss psychologist, Carl Jung. According to Jung, archetypes are elements, pictures or motifs within the collective unconscious of humanity. He deduced their existence based on years of behavioral studies, dreams, and common symbols found within art, myths and religions worldwide.

Jung believed that in literature and films characters can seem instantly familiar to us because elements of their personalities are primal and archetypal—a part of our shared collective unconscious. Archetypes represent a pattern of ideas that are timeless and symbolize basic human motivations, values and characteristics.

Some marketers believe that successful brands with a strong sense of identity may have an unconscious association, by their audiences, with archetypal qualities. They claim that when a leader identifies the archetype or archetypes that are most like their own personality, they can emphasize these aspects of their brand identity and personal story to create a stronger unconscious appeal with their audience.

Similarly, if a thought leader identifies complementary archetypal personalities among their audiences and mirrors the hopes and aspirations of those individuals through their communications, then that leader can potentially increase both their brand recognition and top-of-mind awareness.

WHAT IS YOUR ARCHETYPAL PERSONALITY?

INSTRUCTIONS: Review these Brand Archetype descriptions and identify your top three (3). Look at your existing brand and find opportunities to bring any archetypal aspects of your personality into your brand.

HERO

INNOCENT

CITIZEN

CAREGIVER

REBEL

MAGICIAN

SAGE

LOVER

CREATOR

JESTER

EXPLORER

SOVEREIGN

BRAND ARCHETYPES

// The Hero—also called the superhero or the warrior. The hero's desire is to prove his or her worth and leadership position. The core qualities of the hero include quality, efficiency, reliability and being number one.

// The Innocent—also considered the romantic. Its core qualities are wholesome, pure, natural, safe, clean, free and happy.

// The Citizen—also called the everyman or the regular average guy. The qualities of this archetype are to belong, integrity, fairness, equity and responsibility to its community.

// The Caregiver—also called the parent, the nurturer or the altruist. The core qualities of this archetype are its unselfish concern and devotion to nurture and care for others.

// The Rebel—also called the outlaw or the revolutionary. The core qualities are change, being free-spirited, brave, a part of the counter-culture, and a rule breaker.

// The Magician—also called the shaman or the visionary. The core qualities are a desire for the understanding of the universe and how it works. It is spiritual, holistic, and a visionary that sometimes works miracles.

// The Sage—also called the scholar, the guru, the thinker, the philosopher or the teacher. The sage seeks truth and wisdom in all things. It is wise, open-minded, an expert, objective and autonomous, interested in substance over style and facts over speculation.

// The Lover—also called the idealist or the dreamer. This archetype desires passion, sensuality, is indulgent in matters of the senses, and has a sexy sense of style.

// The Creator—also called the artist. The creator represents imagination, expressiveness, a willingness to take risks, and is a cultural pioneer with a developed sense of the aesthetic.

// The Jester—also called the joker, the fool or the comedian. This archetype desires playfulness, spontaneity, is impulsive, fun, lives in the moment, is carefree and offers a unique perspective on truth and reality.

// The Explorer—also called the seeker or the wanderer. Its core qualities include a desire for adventure, excitement and discovery. It is self-directed, innovative, an individualist and a traveler.

// The Sovereign—also called the ruler, the king or the leader. Its desire is for power and control. It is decisive, stable, and enjoys being in charge.

The Benefits of Archetypal Branding

By identifying the archetype in your personal brand, theoretically you can amplify the impact of your brand by resonating with a familiar personality type in your audiences' unconscious. The archetype provides a guideline for how thought leaders can emphasize their authentic qualities to stand out and be better recognized.

Brand archetypes are built on values and these values will resonate with specific audiences. Shared values promote trust and build relationships over time. A trusted brand identity that represents a familiar archetype can potentially gain an advantage in creating top-of-mind awareness and expand a leader's reach and recognition.

MY TOP 3 ARCHETYPES:

// ARCHETYPE:

// ARCHETYPE:

// ARCHETYPE:

"AUTHENTICITY IS OUR NATURAL STATE OF BEING. THE AUTHENTIC SELF IS A STATE OF BEING WHERE WE ARE CENTERED, CREATIVE, ADAPTIVE, AND INSPIRED."
— HENNA INAM, WIRED FOR AUTHENTICITY

M.E.S.S.A.G.I.N.G.

Beyond what they read, what you say and how you say it comprises what your audience hears and what they think (and feel) about you. Your message can either make you stand out or remain lost in the crowd.

ME – ME	E – ELEVATOR	S-SIMPLIFY
Share you and your unique personality through your messaging.	Having a short informative pitch helps others understand what you do and why.	Having a single message helps with consistency and clarity.

S – SINCERE	A – AUDIENCE	G – GET CONSISTENT
Be you. Don't allow messages to be sent out that do not represent you or your organization.	Be mindful of your audience. Adjust your message to the audience you are talking to.	Make sure your messaging is consistent. Mixed messages can lead to confusion among followers.

I – INTERNAL	N – NEEDS	G – GOOD
Look to your core values to develop your messaging.	Speak to (and understand) what problems your audience needs to solve.	Get really good at presenting your stand out statement. Practice. Practice. Practice.

STORYTELLING AND "STORYSELLING"

Great stories have heroes. They have villains and they have conflict. They may have happy endings, sad endings or sometimes no ending at all. Bruce Springsteen, the Boss, has painted pictures for decades of the American experience through his music and lyrics. Each of his songs tells a story and these stories have the power to touch us as if he's talking about our lives, or someone we know.

Storytelling is as old as human communication. It's how lessons and news were communicated in the past. Humans are hard-wired to listen to stories and learn from them. Great storytelling brings people together to share an experience, making a single individual a part of something bigger. Then, when you weave your ideas or solution into a story, it simply becomes an accepted part of the story line.

EVERY STORY YOU TELL CONTINUES TO BUILD YOUR VALUE.

Your personal brand, whether you know it or not, is made up of stories—your stories and the stories others tell about you. Your story is more than what you tell people, it's also what they believe about you based on their experience of interacting with your ideas, solutions or other communications.

Your story is more than a catchy speech title. It's rooted in your own experiences and your purpose (we keep coming back to that don't we?). This is why authenticity is such an important part of your story—what you say must ring true with your audience or you lose credibility and trust.

As Bruce Springsteen is to storytelling for entertainment, Steve Jobs is to storytelling for corporations. Jobs presented information to a corporate audience in an entertaining way—as a story. He was famous for his keynote addresses to announce new products and new innovations. What is not as well known is that he agonized for hours over the details of his presentations. And as a result, he delivered clear, inspiring messages and simple, bold ideas about technology and its ability to change lives.

HOW DO YOU TELL YOUR STORY?

One thing is certain—you can't expect to stand out from the crowd by telling the same story as everyone else. If you want to transform yourself as a leader, you first must transform your story.

Your goal is to think differently about the stories you tell about you or your organization. A good story is authentic, creative, intimate and emotional. It inspires action and takes the audience on a journey with you and your brand. Great stories affect the way we feel, the way we think and how we behave.

To tell your story, first know who you are. Your story's main character (you) has a personality. What's it like? Write down some of your qualities and create a personality profile to refer to and remember. Does your personality have characteristics like any of the known archetypes you identified?

Identify who you are—honestly, authentically and openly. Make the main character of your story someone that your followers can relate to and identify with—a character with similar values, goals and aspirations. This can transform your story and your storytelling. And if you're promoting a solution or service, your storytelling can become *story-selling*.

CONSISTENCY BUILDS BRANDS.

Another important thing thought leaders can learn from Steve Jobs is to maintain consistency in one's storytelling style. It's not just the words you speak, but how you look and how you project when you are telling your story. If you are the leader within an organization, your stories must align with the story of your organization. If they don't, there will be a disconnect and they will lack authenticity. Your organization's story must be genuine and in sync with you and your personal story. And the style of your presentation must also be genuine, honest and reflect who you are, or it won't ring true.

// STEPHEN COVEY

Stephen Covey was educator, businessman and keynote speaker as well as author of several best-selling books, the most popular of which was "The Seven Habits of Highly Effective People," in which he promotes "the character ethic: of aligning one's values with universal and timeless principles. A key influence on his thinking was his study of American self-help books done for his doctoral dissertation. He established the Covey Leadership Center that merged in 1997 with Franklin Quest to form Franklin Covey, a publisher and provider of leadership, individual effectiveness, and business assessment services.

Stephen Covey's Stand Out Statement:

I help others identify the principles of leadership. Personal leadership is the process of keeping your vision and values before you and aligning your life with them.

YOUR BRAND, WHETHER YOU KNOW IT OR NOT, IS MADE UP OF STORIES—**YOUR STORIES AND THE STORIES OTHERS TELL ABOUT YOU. YOUR STORY IS MORE THAN WHAT YOU TELL PEOPLE,** IT IS ALSO WHAT THEY BELIEVE ABOUT YOU BASED ON THEIR EXPERIENCE OF INTERACTING WITH YOU—**IT'S ROOTED IN YOUR VALUES, YOUR EXPERIENCES, YOUR ACTIONS AND WHO YOU ARE.**

CREATING A BRAND PERSONALITY

To make your brand story relevant and interesting, the characters in your story should reflect the personalities and social characteristics of your audience. Research on population segments can identify detailed qualities and activities of different segments, providing valuable information on their lifestyles, habits, preferences, education, buying patterns, and even where they live.

With this detailed lifestyle data about your audience, use characters in your brand story that will make psychological connections with them. When your story messages and images can reflect the values, personality, and lifestyle preferences of your audience, they'll feel more involved with your brand. And ultimately, relating to your ideas or solutions becomes an obvious choice as an extension of your story.

The key to success with the storytelling strategy is authenticity—aligning what you communicate about yourself with the truth of who and what you are. If your attempt to portray yourself is just a façade, a mask for who and what you are, then your storytelling attempts to create an appealing personality will eventually fail.

SO HOW CAN YOU MAKE YOUR BRAND MORE DISTINCT FROM OTHERS?

The answer is simple. Tell the truth, the whole truth and nothing but. Explain to your audience who you are and what you stand for. Instead of trying to argue that you possess certain qualities that they should consider important, show them what attributes and characteristics you do have and let them decide.

By being honest, you do not have to convince anyone that you are something else. By authenticating your messaging, you will stand out from your peers and your competition as being uniquely you.

PERSONAL BRAND ATTRIBUTES

Take 15 minutes to write down the attributes that your audience would use to describe you:

_____

_____

_____

_____

_____

_____

_____

_____

_____

_____

"BE YOURSELF. EVERYONE ELSE IS TAKEN."
— OSCAR WILDE

BE PREPARED (TO TELL YOUR STORY).

The Boy Scout motto, "Be Prepared," devised in 1907, is about more than tying intricate knots and building campfires in the wilderness. It means to "always be in a state of readiness in mind and body to be able to respond quickly in any situation."

To an emerging thought leader this motto is especially relevant today. Being prepared means that you become so familiar and comfortable with your topic and the words you use to describe it that it becomes automatic to explain what you do and what you stand for *whenever* the opportunity presents itself.

Becoming a thought leader is like training for a marathon. You build your abilities to the point where you can "be prepared" to respond effectively and deliver a summary of your overall message to anyone, in five seconds, five minutes or fifty minutes. And like a marathon trainee, with consistent practice and focus, you will develop your skills to the point that you are always in a state of readiness, in mind and body, so your response to any opportunity to share your ideas becomes second nature.

Have you ever had that dream where you find yourself on center stage and can't remember your lines? Everyone is staring at you and recording everything you do and say. You're not prepared and stage fright begins to take over.

In today's world, this nightmare often becomes a reality. Everything you say communicates the story of your brand. Yet, you never know who is recording what you say and when you say it. And once your words are out in the world, you can't take them back.

The only way to stay ahead of this reality is to be prepared and be consistent. When you're on that stage and in the spotlight, choose your words wisely and make sure they are true.

5-25-50-100-500—A preparedness exercise. Write five versions of your message in five different lengths—in 5 words, 25 words, 50 words, 100 words and 500 words. You might find that each version will lay a foundation for the next, each one allowing you to go into greater detail about your topic or area of expertise. Once you've completed these, read them each day. Memorize them. Edit them if necessary to further hone your message until you get the most simple, direct, accurate and authentic statement of what you do and why from 5 words to 500 words in length.

The elevator speech. To understand the importance of knowing what you stand for, try this. Step into an elevator and ask someone what they do. They will say something like "I am in business development for the XYZ Widget Company. We make widgets for businesses all over the state." Now ask them what they stand for. You will probably get silence and a shrug.

Picture yourself in this situation. You're in an elevator at a convention among your followers and peers and someone asks, "What do you stand for?" What do you say? You've got about 15 seconds to establish yourself and make an impression. The person listening won't even be tuned in to the first 10 seconds because they are judging your appearance and analyzing their gut feelings about you. So, you've really got only five seconds. Can you say what you stand for in five seconds? **One one-thousand, two one-thousand, three one-thousand, four one-thousand, five one-thousand and you're done**. If you had practiced the 5-25-50-100-500 exercise described above, you would be ready.

5-25-50-100-500

5-25-50-100-500 EXERCISE: Write five versions of your message in five different lengths.

5

25

50

100

500

ELEVATOR SPEECH

ELEVATOR SPEECH EXERCISE: Start with the structure—What the world needs / What you provide / Where or how others don't or won't.

// WHAT MAKES YOU DISTINCT

// ONE WORD

(problem your stand out statement solves)

I

(your distinct advantage)

SO

(key benefit)

UNLIKE

(other thought leaders)

"AFTER A PRESENTATION,
63% OF ATTENDEES
REMEMBER STORIES.
ONLY 5% REMEMBER
STATISTICS."
— CHIP & DAN HEATH

LOOK, LISTEN, LEARN

We know that social marketing is a two-way dialogue between an individual and their audiences. Using social media effectively is like entering a conversation already in progress. People are talking, possibly about you or your area of expertise. Before entering, you should listen to get a sense of what's already being said. Before entering, you should listen to get a sense of what's already being said.

After this "listening" research, make a list of what you've found. Then refer to this list to remind you what people are saying and how social media can help guide these conversations towards what you want to "hear."

Now that you know what's already being said, set goals determining what you want to achieve using social media. What are your current communications objectives? What new ones would you like to accomplish? The key is to *integrate* social media into your communications plan, not let it take over entirely. Each message that you post with social media should reflect your objectives and help you meet your goals.

To ensure the best visibility and reach, you need to choose the right social networking sites. Each social media tool has something different to offer and is useful for different purposes. There are many options, so after some research on the benefits of each, make your selection, but also make sure you understand the rationale for your choices.

HOW DO ONLINE COMMUNICATIONS FIT IN WITH YOUR OVERALL MESSAGING?

Your brand identity and presence online are a large part of your overall messaging strategy. People used to pick up the yellow pages to look for an individual, a business or service. Today, they use search engines to find information and reviews about people, places, products and services. But don't stop there. Search web forums and read comments containing what people are saying about your field of expertise and others working in the same field. Try to understand what they're saying and why they're saying it. Look at the situation as they would. What insights do you gain from this? With the knowledge of these new insights, you can adjust your social marketing strategy or brand messaging to present you and your ideas in the best light.

// MALCOLM GLADWELL Journalist, author and

public speaker, Gladwell is a thought leader in the field of research in the social sciences and the unexpected implications of that research. His book, The Tipping Point has become a widely quoted and accepted idea in conventional wisdom. He has been a staff writer for the New Yorker magazine since 1996.

Malcolm Gladwell's Stand Out Statement:

I offer insights about life as a human being, the value of hard work and perseverance to realize and achieve your dreams.

SEARCH TERMS

SEARCH TERMS EXERCISE: Search for topics that are aligned with what you do and how you stand out.

// TOP KEY TERMS

BRAND ATTRIBUTES

PROBLEM/SOLUTION EXERCISE: What problems do you solve? What solutions do you provide? Draw a line connecting each problem to a solution. Look for areas where they don't align.

// PROBLEMS I SOLVE

_____

_____

_____

_____

_____

_____

_____

_____

_____

_____

// SOLUTIONS I PROVIDE

_____

_____

_____

_____

_____

_____

_____

_____

_____

AUTHENTICITY IN BRIEF:

// Authenticity is expressed primarily through words and proven through actions.

// Your words (message) should honestly reflect who you are and what you represent.

// Your Stand Out Statement is a short one-sentence expression of the why behind what you say and do and how it benefits the world.

// Your brand "voice" is a combination of the words you choose and the style of how you express those words—verbally and in writing.

// Your brand voice should be authentic and true to who you are—distinctive and recognizable and an extension of your purpose.

// Using stories in your communications can help people relate, understand and remember your message.

// Be prepared to explain what you do and why in as little as five seconds (your elevator speech).

// Social media is a two-way dialogue that requires different communication skills.

TAKE ACTION:

☐ In 25 words or less, describe how what you do in the world is an honest and authentic expression of your heart's deepest desire.

☐ Take one of your life experiences and write it into a story that you would share with an audience in your next presentation.

☐ Describe two life experiences that you feel define who you are and why you do what you do.

DO YOU **TARGET YOUR KEY MESSAGE** TO YOUR CORE AUDIENCE OR ARE YOU COMMUNICATING TO EVERYONE THE SAME WAY? **HOW'S THAT WORKING?**

I HAVE **A CONSISTENT FLOW OF NEW FOLLOWERS** THAT ARE WELL DEFINED, NURTURED AND MANAGED.

AUDIENCE

// IDENTIFY WHERE YOU STAND.

Which of these statements most accurately reflects your situation with generating new followers?

- ☐ I do not have a consistent flow of new followers.
- ☐ I somewhat have a consistent flow of new followers.
- ☐ I have a consistent flow of new followers, but they are not segmented compared to my core audience.
- ☐ I have a consistent flow of new followers, and they are defined but they are not nurtured or managed.
- ☐ I have a consistent flow of new followers, and they are defined, nurtured and managed.

WHAT'S YOUR IDEAL FOLLOWER PROFILE? A potential follower who fits your ideal audience description and is interested in what you have to say. This person sees value in your ideas or solutions and can appreciate the differences that you offer compared to your peers or competitors.

Thought leaders are not born, they are made. Often, they emerge from within their field as individuals with a particular knowledge or expertise, a unique insight, energy or passion, *and the capacity or ability to influence others through their communications*. These people build an audience in their distinct niche through their authenticity, the truth, relevance and timeliness of their message, and the power and appeal of their personality. They create the idea map for others to follow and share.

Where you have thought leaders there are thought followers. They are the people who repeat, retweet, restate and share a thought leader's ideas and communications. By empathizing with a thought leader's ideas and message, they gain a sense of being part of something greater than themselves. By sharing these ideas to a wider audience, they describe to others who they are and what they feel or believe in.

We are all thought followers at one time or another. Spreading and expanding on good ideas is important and necessary. The enthusiasm expressed through sharing a thought leader's message to their circle of friends and followers makes thought followers an essential part of a thought leader's growth and expands a thought leader's message.

There has never been a more ideal time to build an audience for your idea or solution. But with so many people competing for attention online and offline, it is also harder than ever to "stand out" from the crowd. The solution to setting yourself apart in such a noisy crowded world, as we've stated in the previous chapter, is to develop your "authentic voice."

GROWING AN AUDIENCE IS ABOUT MORE THAN CHASING FOLLOWERS; IT'S ABOUT STANDING OUT SO THAT YOU DRAW FOLLOWERS TO YOU.

Authenticity is like magic. One goal of doing the work to develop your authentic voice is that your words and ideas are based on a deep knowledge of who you are and what you stand for and not on some invention. An audience recognizes honesty, intuitively and realistically, and that builds trust in the speaker and in his or her message. Truth and authenticity resonate with those people within an audience who will be attracted to the speaker and motivated to becoming thought followers.

Leadership and followership are two sides of a coin. Leaders need followers. Motivated and effective followers can shape a thought leader's behavior and message by asking for greater clarity. Followers can encourage a thought leader to delve deeper into their subject area and even inspire new insights or solutions. The influence is reciprocal.

Who are your ideal thought followers? This question is an issue of quality over quantity. For some thought leaders this may require a new perspective on audience building. If you measure the effectiveness of your audience-building process only on the number of new followers you attract, then it's likely that you are spending a lot of time focused only on the size of your audience and not those that fit your "ideal" thought follower profile.

You can have more from less. Bringing in fewer new followers can be beneficial. Slow growth can mean you are attracting more loyal and informed followers who understand and resonate with you and your message. Fast growth can mean new followers are responding only to one idea or presentation you've made that has gone "viral" and created a temporary bump of interest.

Reaching new followers through targeted communications. This is a good place to begin to define your ideal new thought follower. What things do your current followers have in common? What attributes of their demographics are similar and what are different? Add this information to your ideal new follower profile and expand from there. By surveying your existing followers, you might learn what attracted them to your message in the first place. Understanding who your ideal prospective followers are and building a strategy to attract similar individuals will help improve the efficiency of audience building efforts.

Listen to your followers—Listen more closely to what your followers say. Survey or interview them to learn what they feel is important or valuable about your ideas or solutions. Discover what they like and dislike. What you learn could help improve the way you communicate and even show you what new potential followers might look like. In the process, you may gather positive comments and testimonials that can help build your credibility and visibility.

Your current universe of followers contains your best most loyal thought followers and promoters. Thank them for following you, reward them for their loyalty and they'll keep coming back. Tom Peters, well-known writer and lecturer on excellence in business practices, says, "The magic formula that successful businesses have discovered is to treat customers like guests and employees like people." This formula applies equally to thought leaders and their followers.

See yourself through your audience's eyes. Take a fresh look at your ideas or solutions from your audience's perspective. Think less about why you feel your solution is special, and more about what your followers feel is important. What are the real strengths of your ideas? What are the benefits in the eyes of your audience? Benefits describe how your ideas or solutions improve your followers' lives. Benefits include convenience, ease, and saving time or money. Benefits say how your solution satisfies real customer needs and desires. Benefits are emotion-based. According to the website, entrepreneur.com, benefits answer your followers' question "How does this help me?" Does your message identify what's in it for your followers and their well-being? Make sure you spell out the benefits in all your communications.

// ARIANNA HUFFINGTON A syndicated columnist,

author of 15 books, and businesswoman, Arianna Huffington is co-founder of the *Huffington Post* (HuffPost) and founder and CEO of *Thrive Global*, a company that offers science-based solutions to end stress and burnout. In 2016, The Huffington Post became the first commercially run US digital media enterprise to win a Pulitzer Prize. Also in 2016, she was named to Oprah Winfrey's *SuperSoul100* list of visionaries and influential leaders.

Arianna Huffington's Stand Out Statement:

We think, mistakenly, that success is the result of the amount of time we put in at work, instead of the quality of time we put in. I focus my work with others on quality.

AUDIENCE TYPES

This graphic shows the steps of people becoming more familiar with you and the ideas or solutions you offer.

// **Stranger**—Someone completely unfamiliar with you and your message

// **Audience**—Someone who is a reader or listener of your speech, presentation, book, website, or research paper

// **Connections**—People who are familiar with you and your message and who have agreed to be connected to you

// **Thought Followers**—People who regularly follow your messages, blog posts, or presentations of new content

// **Promoters**—People who not only follow you but also share and promote your message with others

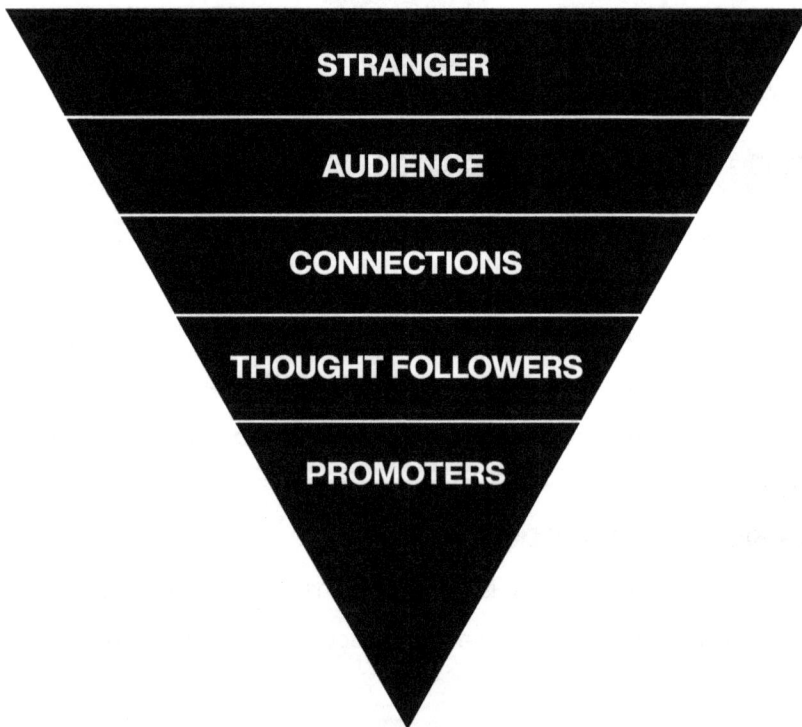

STRANGER

AUDIENCE

CONNECTIONS

THOUGHT FOLLOWERS

PROMOTERS

AUDIENCE TYPES

INSTRUCTIONS: Briefly describe how you would communicate differently to each of these groups.

// **STRANGERS:**

// **AUDIENCE:**

// **CONNECTIONS:**

// THOUGHT FOLLOWERS:

// PROMOTERS:

YOUR IDEAL FOLLOWER PROFILE

The first step in creating a regular flow of new followers is to agree on a set of criteria of what an ideal follower looks like, then develop a communications plan that makes certain your communications reach those people. The following are examples of information that you may include in your profile.

☐ A set of demographics that includes areas of interest or job field

☐ A day in their lives

☐ A list of their pain points, motivations and goals

☐ Where do they look for information?

Your research will allow you to refine your audience profile over time and make it clear what qualities and characteristics best identify your true ideal prospects. Once you understand what your followers are like and what motivates them, you can develop communications directed to them—information they are looking for to solve problems or overcome specific challenges in their lives. The more information you can provide, the more helpful you can be. Providing them with useful information builds trust so that when they think of someone who stands out in a particular field, you are top-of-mind. This is growth through attraction, growth through relationship building.

Once you establish a relationship, you can identify where a prospective follower is in your audience growth plan. This enables you to develop more targeted communications that fit these new followers.

IDEAL FOLLOWER BRAINSTORM

IDEAL FOLLOWER BRAINSTORM: Put on your thinking cap and analyze your ideal followers, the motivations and challenges they face professionally and personally and how you might do a better job of providing value to them and their lives.

// **WHO ARE THEY:**

// **WHERE THEY ARE:**

// **WHAT'S IMPORTANT TO THEM:**

// **WHAT KEEPS THEM UP AT NIGHT:**

LOVE THE "ONES" YOU'RE WITH

It's important to give a lot of love to your audience. Much of what you would do to nurture a personal relationship can be applied to your thought follower relationships. Your online activity can generate new followers who need "love" and nurturing, just like any other relationship. What can you do to love new followers and turn them into loyal and positive influencers?

Check out this list of best practices:

// Know your audience. Different activities attract different audiences. When you develop a communications campaign, tailor your message to match certain characteristics of your projected audience. Don't try to communicate the same to everyone.

// Deliver what you promise. What was your initial value proposition to your audience? If you promised something by a specific date, then follow-through and deliver it by that date. If you did not include a specific timeline, deliver on your promise in a reasonable amount of time. Don't keep your audience waiting.

// Be accessible and available. Your audience may have questions or want more information about something you've said or written. You need to be accessible, through email or phone, with answers. Have a plan to respond to audience questions within a "reasonable" amount of time—then explain on your online presence specifically how long someone can expect to receive a response to their questions.

// Schedule regular interactions. Much like a weekly or monthly date night, your audience needs to have a regularly scheduled interaction with you, whether it's through email, a zoom meeting call, or something else. Determine a "balanced" schedule of these interactions that shows consistency but doesn't overwhelm your followers with a barrage of constant communications.

*// **Be unique and valuable.*** What can you offer your leads that they can't get anywhere else? What offer can you provide that holds value for them? The more unique and valuable your offers are, the more reasons your audience will have to follow and continue a relationship with you.

CLASSIFYING NEW FOLLOWERS

*// **Preferred passenger***: This is an ideal follower, someone who fits with your values and point of view. They have the potential of becoming a healthy two-way relationship (you provide value to them, and they provide value to you through their loyalty and referrals). You want to spend most of your time focusing on these audience members.

*// **Frequent flyers***: These are your long-term relationships (and also preferred passengers). They are loyal. They influence others and provide referrals. They need to be nurtured.

*// **Stowaways:*** These individuals are high maintenance. They require more of your energy and attention and offer low value to you.

*// **Cargo***: These individuals weigh your thought leadership efforts down. Interacting with them can require an inordinate amount of your time that you could be spending with your preferred passengers. Be polite, they are simply needy and do not offer a return value for your time and energy. An equal exchange of energy is the best balance in any relationship.

"EVERYONE IS NOT YOUR CUSTOMER."
— SETH GODIN

AUDIENCE PERSONA MAP

AUDIENCE PERSONA MAP: Create a map for each follower persona you record.

// NAME:

// MAIN INTERESTS:

// KEY ISSUES AND RESPONSIBILITIES:

// PERSONAL PROFILE:

// WHAT MAKES LIFE HARD:

// WHAT MAKES LIFE FUN:

AUDIENCE IN BRIEF:

// Every thought leader has thought followers—people who find the thought leader's message appealing and who share the thought leader's ideas and values.

// There has never been a better time to connect with an audience and build a following.

// To grow your followers, first define your ideal follower and direct your communications to others who fit that definition and profile.

Q: Do you know who your followers are and why they are interested in your message?

Q: Do you know the best method and media to reach new potential followers?

TAKE ACTION:

☐ Ask your followers to provide feedback on the most important thing you do or say that made them choose to follow you.

☐ Ask them how often they would like to hear from you and what they would like to know more about.

IF WE FOCUS ON WHAT MAKES EACH OF US DISTINCT, OUR AUDIENCE WOULD NOT BE CONFUSED BY EVERYTHING **LOOKING THE SAME.**

STANDING OUT AMONG YOUR PEERS, INFLUENCERS AND OTHER THOUGHT LEADERS.

DISTINCTION

// IDENTIFY WHERE YOU STAND.

Which of these statements most accurately reflects the current level that you stand out among your peers, influencers and other thought leaders?

- ☐ I do not stand out.
- ☐ I am not clear on how or if I stand out.
- ☐ I stand out, but I do not consistently communicate why and how I stand out.
- ☐ I stand out among my peers, but I do not stand out to outside influencers and thought leaders.
- ☐ I stand out among my peers, influencers and other thought leaders.

DISTINCTION: the difference or contrast between similar things or people; positive qualities that set you apart from others. The secret to gaining distinction is by being more of who you are, operating from a foundation based on purpose, and communicating from a position of confidence about the benefit your idea or solution offers to people's lives. **HOW CAN YOU ACCOMPLISH THIS?**

When Lorrie and I were children, each morning our mother would lay out our clothes on a green "pleather" chair in our living room. You know those plastic leather chairs that were popular back in the 70s? The ones that if you fell asleep on them, your face would stick to the fake leather. Well, each morning we'd get up and get dressed for school and our outfits for the day would be sitting on that green pleather chair and they were always exactly alike.

I never could figure out why she dressed us the same. But as a result, most people knew us as the "little twins." I guess it was considered cute. They would say, "Look, there go the little twins." They didn't even know our names, only that we were twins.

Our grandmother made most of our clothes, so maybe it was easier to simply make two sets of everything rather than sewing separate clothes for the two of us. Maybe they didn't want to show any preference for either one by picking out different outfits. Maybe it was their way of emphasizing the special relationship that twins share. I'm not sure, but I can say with certainty that it makes it very hard to stand out and be noticed as an individual when you always look exactly like somebody else.

I didn't think about it much until I was almost 13. Around that time, I remember clearly that looking and being different from my twin sister was just about the most important thing in my world. I wanted to be seen as a separate and distinct person. And when you've been one-half of the little twins for 13 years, you must make some dramatic changes to alter that perception.

So that's what I did. I dressed as differently as I could, which back in those days meant I wore black a lot. I cut my hair differently, I hung out with other people who were trying to be different as well—artists, musicians and other experimental types who for one reason or another were trying to find or create their own identities. What I learned was that most of what I did to be different was external. I was trading being part of one group (the twins) with being part of another, larger group (creative types).

Most of us in that group wanted to be recognized for our differences—the unique qualities that made us special and helped us stand out from everyone else. It took me years of trying to be something or someone else before I grasped this important truth—the shortest road to being different is to be more of who I am.

SPOT THE DIFFERENCE

DISTINCTION EXERCISE: Can you spot the differences that make these similar images distinct one from the other?

YOUR MOST DISTINGUISHING CHARACTERISTICS

Identifying the characteristics that distinguish you from anyone else has never been more essential for standing out than today. The global mediascape has drawn events and people into international focus. With expanded exposure comes expanded challenges and opportunities. If a person, and especially a thought leader, does not tell his or her own story, someone else will tell it for them.

In the process of standing out, you learn to define and communicate your purpose (who you are) and what you stand for. And you make your purpose a focus of your communications and continued growth (what you do). Next you explore your brand personality to find out which parts best represent the strengths and memorable qualities of the main character of your brand story (your story). All these steps can establish and direct how you can get noticed, remembered and distinguished in the social and cultural environment of today.

What characteristic is **UNIQUE TO YOU** that you can leverage to **PROMOTE YOUR BRAND AND STAND OUT?**

YOUR DISTINCT ADVANTAGE IS NOT JUST WHAT MAKES YOU DIFFERENT, IT MAKES THE IDEAS OR SOLUTION THAT YOU OFFER DIFFERENT AS WELL—**IT IS WHAT YOU STAND FOR. IT IS THE UNIQUE COMBINATION OF TALENTS, EXPERIENCES, CULTURE, STORIES, SKILLS AND INCLINATIONS** THAT MAKE UP WHO YOU ARE AND WHAT YOU DO IN WAYS THAT OTHERS DON'T, CAN'T AND WON'T.

AUTHENTICITY AND YOUR DISTINCT ADVANTAGE

In the process of communicating about their ideas or solutions, it's typical for an individual to overlook "authenticity" in favor of things that they believe are more attention grabbing—clever messages, drama, flashy events, and the showy use of design elements. And yet authenticity is the very thing that will build trust within relationships and keeps followers coming back again and again.

Under the Brand Traffic Control™ process, you'll learn that the things that authentically distinguish you from others have greater alignment to your vision, values, beliefs and purpose. When you align your activities with your purpose and authentic personality, you operate from a position of confidence and strength. Your distinct advantage is not just what makes you different, it's what can make your message different as well.

Identifying your purpose (why you do what you do and what difference that makes to your audience) takes some soul searching to pin down, but it is well worth the effort.

Ultimately, your distinct advantage is where what you offer aligns with the distinct beliefs, views and needs of your audience in a way that others don't, can't or won't. Instead of trying to be all things to all people, your purpose and your distinct advantage help you get "pointy"—more focused on who you are and what message you're trying to communicate.

Instead of trying to be all things to all people, **YOUR PURPOSE AND YOUR DISTINCT ADVANTAGE HELP YOU** get "pointy" on who you are and what you're trying to do.

When you say, "this is what I stand for and this is why I do what I do," you do so with the understanding that you will appeal most to those people who share your values and who relate to what you say you stand for. But that's okay, because those people are your ideal followers—potentially your most loyal followers and ultimately your brand ambassadors.

DISTINGUISH YOURSELF. BECOME A THOUGHT LEADER.

When you create consistent and genuine communications that align with your core values, beliefs, and purpose, you will stand out and take off. Having a great idea or solution is not enough to distinguish yourself in the world today—and marketing alone won't get the attention and loyalty of an audience to support the sustained growth and acceptance of your ideas or solutions.

You are a leader and leaders think like leaders. To distinguish yourself from the crowd, take the next step—stand up and stand out as a thought leader in your field, whatever field that may be.

LEARN TO READ YOUR AUDIENCE

Whenever you're giving a public presentation, it's important to watch your audience carefully and assess their attention level, or "check the audience's pulse" to help you understand how they are responding to what you're saying. An audience is made up of a mix of people who likely don't all have the same interests, have different attention spans and varying perspectives on the topic of your talk. Maintaining eye contact and reading body language signals can help you understand how engaged they are and whether they are responding positively or negatively to you and your presentation.

// Eye contact—As you're scanning the faces of your audience does their eye contact with you indicate if they are interested or not in what you're saying? With some practice, you can learn to see, hear and even feel the energy of an engaged and open group and know that you're connecting with them.

// Reading the signs—An engaged group of people will also show body language signals such as smiling and nodding their heads, leaning forward and looking intent and interested, returning your eye contact, laughing at your jokes, asking questions or taking notes. These signals give you feedback that you're on track and in sync with your audience and that they're interested and involved. But what happens when the signs change, the energy in the room begins to drop and your audience becomes quiet and withdrawn?

Some signs that you're losing your audience's attention or that they disapprove or disagree with what you're saying might include people whispering with their neighbors and not paying attention, looking around, frowning, crossing their arms and legs and leaning back in their chairs, and even checking their cellphones, watches, or nervously fidgeting with glasses, pens or earrings. Then you know it's time to shift gears and turn up the heat in your talk.

// **Keeping your audience engaged**—As a speaker, it's your job to be thoroughly prepared and well-rehearsed so that you can shift gears and adapt to changing interest levels in your audience. Remember that you are both educating and entertaining this group on your chosen topic. If you know your material and have practiced your delivery, you will be able to adapt your message and behavior to give your audience a reason to listen—share a personal story; ask a provocative question; state a fact that's amusing, extraordinary, or troubling; offer a humorous observation or anecdote. Sharing something personal is always engaging and gives you the opportunity to show that you are vulnerable and human. Remember, vulnerability is powerful.

"In a live performance, it's a collaboration with the audience; you **RIDE THE EBB AND FLOW OF THE CROWD'S ENERGY.** On screen, you don't have that."
— Jon Batiste

THE 10,000 HOUR RULE

Malcolm Gladwell, an English-born journalist, author and public speaker, is often misquoted as saying that it takes 10,000 hours of practice to become an expert at something. In his book, *Outliers: The Story of Success*, Gladwell actually said, "you need 10,000 hours to become a phenom," which applies more to the path of becoming a thought leader than an expert.

Yes, becoming a thought leader is not an overnight process, though to someone on the outside, it may look like someone stands out suddenly, as if out of nowhere. But you can bet there are lots of hours of work behind that rise into public awareness. To become a phenom—such an awesome stand out that your first name is enough to tell people who you are and what you stand for, could take longer than you think. And you can bet that journey takes a few hours, or a few hundred hours, or...

WHAT DO YOU WANT TO BE KNOWN FOR?

To identify your distinct advantage, look beyond what you say to how you say it and "what you want to be known for." This last quality is your stake in the ground. For example: "This is what I've learned, what I know is true, and what I offer as a solution—I believe it's important because it can make peoples' lives better, stop global warming, and create world peace." Well, maybe your ideas or solutions won't do all those things, but you get the picture.

IDENTIFY YOUR DISTINCT ADVANTAGE

DISTINCT ADVANTAGE QUALITIES: What does your audience want that you offer, and others don't? Use findings to identify your distinct advantages in this section.

// WHAT PEOPLE WANT:	// WHAT YOU PROVIDE:

// WHAT OTHER THOUGHT LEADERS OFFER:

WHAT YOUR AUDIENCE WANTS FROM YOU

DISTINCT ADVANTAGE EXERCISE: What do your followers want that you provide and others don't? Use your findings from the qualities of Distinct Advantage.

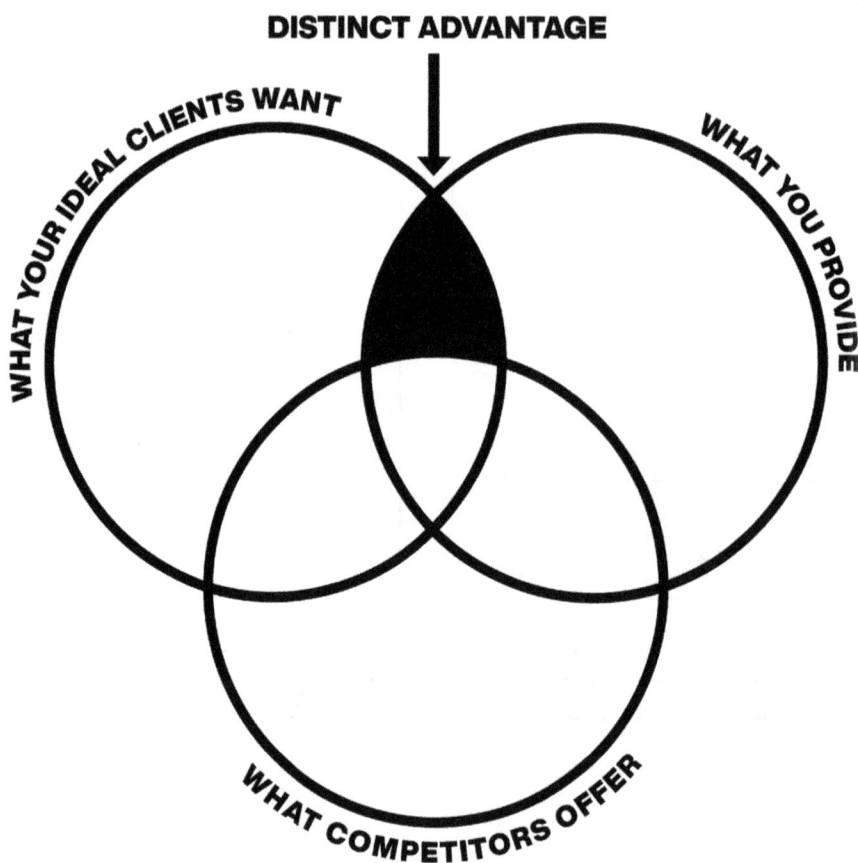

DISTINCT ADVANTAGE

WHAT YOUR IDEAL CLIENTS WANT

WHAT YOU PROVIDE

WHAT COMPETITORS OFFER

DISTINCT ADVANTAGE SUMMARY

DISTINCT ADVANTAGE SUMMARY: Summarize the results here. Your distinct advantage statement will serve as a component for your Elevator Speech in the Authenticity section.

// **DISTINCT ADVANTAGES:**

// **PRIMARY DISTINCT ADVANTAGE:**

// **DISTINCT ADVANTAGE STATEMENT:**

DISTINCT ADVANTAGE MESSAGING

DISTINCT ADVANTAGE MESSAGING: Summarize the results here. Messaging is the content that is a result of distinct advantage activity and findings.

// PRIMARY MESSAGES:

// RECURRING MESSAGES:

DISTINCTION IN BRIEF:

// The way to be more distinct is by being more of who you are and acting with a sense of purpose and confidence about what you do and why.

// Identifying your distinct advantage is essential to standing out as a thought leader; it is a combination of your skills, talents, experiences, stories and inclinations and describes who you are and what you do in ways that others don't, can't and won't.

// Clever and dramatic messages are less important than authenticity and honesty.

// Your audience is attracted to and relates to your shared values and the relevance of the ideas and solutions you offer.

// To identify your distinct advantage, consider "what you want to be known for."

TAKE ACTION:

☐ In one or two sentences, describe your distinct advantage.

☐ Write one way you can emphasize those values more clearly in your communications to followers.

☐ List the personal values or attributes that you feel are behind your distinct advantage.

WITH **THOUSANDS OF WAYS** TO COMMUNICATE TODAY, THE KEY TO STANDING OUT IS BY ALIGNING COMMUNICATIONS IN A WAY THAT **ACHIEVES GOALS.**

A COMMUNICATIONS STRATEGY
IS IN FORCE AND IS ALIGNED
WITH YOUR GOALS.

STRATEGY

// IDENTIFY WHERE YOU STAND.

Which of these statements most accurately reflects the current
description of your communications or marketing plan?

- ☐ I have no communications or marketing plan.

- ☐ I have somewhat of a communications and marketing plan.

- ☐ I have a communications and marketing plan that is in force, but it
  is not aligned with my goals.

- ☐ I have a communications and marketing plan that is aligned with
  my goals but is not implemented consistently.

- ☐ I have a communications and marketing plan that is in force,
  implemented consistently and is aligned with my goals.

STRATEGY INVOLVES YOUR COMMITMENT TO AN INTEGRATED SET OF GOALS AND ACTIONS. Your communications and brand strategies should sync and support one another. Integrated strategies promote alignment, clarify objectives and priorities and focus your efforts on your goals.

When your growth strategy is aligned with your purpose and brand, you are on course to achieve your goals. Under a traditional advertising and communications model, growth strategies and branding strategies were often separate and did not always interact or support one other. Ideally, when you are working from your purpose, your communications and branding strategies work hand-in-hand. Like purpose, these are integrated and communicated consistently to your audience. When you invest the time to align your brand, strategy and purpose, they build the foundation for successfully staying on course. And when strategy and purpose are combined in a written strategic plan, then you can truly take off.

CREATE A PLAN.

While formulating and adjusting a strategy is an ongoing requirement for standing out and taking off, it will be wasted effort without a plan that defines the steps and actions needed to accomplish your goals and to orchestrate their implementation.

Even so, many thought leaders do not spend the time required on the front end to schedule initiatives and set up milestones to analyze how their plans are evolving toward completion. While long-term strategy may be fluid and subject to such things as societal, economic and political changes, the entry of new innovations, and economic shifts can challenge your ability to adapt to change while achieving interim objectives.

PUT IT IN WRITING.

When you put your plan in writing, you can refer to it later and use it as a baseline from which to measure progress. If it's not written down, you might forget steps or parts that are crucial to where you want to go.

ASSIGN RESPONSIBILITY.

If you're part of a team, let every team member know what role they will play in the plan. Explain the tasks they're expected to perform and when they're expected to complete them (due dates). When team members have a clear picture of their tasks and when they need to complete them, when they're motivated by a shared purpose and a common goal, the entire team can work more efficiently and effectively.

YOU ARE ON COURSE WHEN PURPOSE
ALIGNS WITH BRAND AND STRATEGY

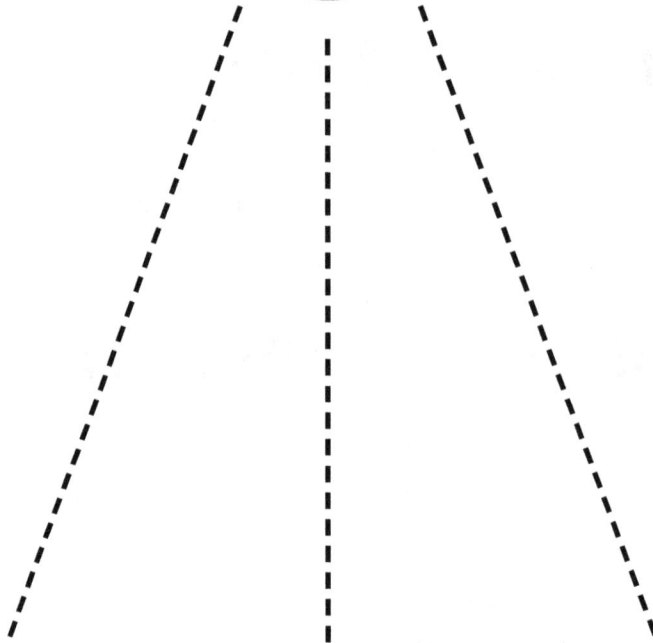

BRAND   PURPOSE   STRATEGY

WHO YOU ARE   **WHY YOU DO**   **YOUR PLAN**
                          WHAT YOU DO   **OF ACTION**

CREATIVE + STRATEGY = HYBRID THINKING

Being twins, we've learned that two heads and two brains are better than one. We use the term "hybrid thinking" to describe the blend of creative thinking and strategic thinking that we bring to the table when discussing solutions with our clients.

Conversations are no longer about whether a brochure should be blue or green, but about who's the target audience? What are their beliefs and needs, and what's the best way to reach them? For years, design was considered a down-stream aspect of business and marketing processes. A product or service would be developed to fill a perceived market need. Then in the final stages, the designer would be called in to create an "attractive package" to make it more appealing to consumers. The important "identity" of the brand was almost an afterthought.

More and more thought leaders we see today benefit from mixing creativity and strategy into a more unified and innovative approach to developing and promoting ideas and solutions. It's a hybrid approach: 50% creative + 50% strategic = 100% effective.

This right brain (creative) and left brain (strategic) approach to communications design blends creative concepts about how a thing should look, feel and sound, and then it shapes, designs and crafts the final form and message into a strategic solution that fills the needs and desires of a specific audience.

Today the creative thinking process goes beyond the visual identity of a brand. According to Tim Brown, the president and CEO of the creative consulting firm IDEO, "... today, if you are developing a marketing strategy, building a new retail space, streamlining a manufacturing operation, or creating a marketing plan to introduce or promote a product or service, your planning is influenced and enhanced by creative thinking." In a presentation to MIT Sloan business students about design and innovation, Brown explained that the creative thinking process is applicable to a wide range of business challenges, from products and services to solutions and ideas.

Brown states that design thinking adds a "human-centered" approach to problem solving. It considers the real needs and wants of people and factors these into the way solutions are communicated, packaged, marketed, supported and maintained. Traditional business thinking ordinarily relies on feature- or function-driven models. Design thinking considers the audience's feelings of satisfaction about the way a solution fulfills their needs and is an integral part of an audience-focused brand strategy.

"GOOD STRATEGIES PROMOTE ALIGNMENT, clarify objectives and priorities and help focus efforts—a commitment to a set of coherent, mutually reinforcing behaviors aimed at achieving specific, competitive goals."
— HBR.com

WHY PLANNING MATTERS

Think about how many times you use the word "plan" in your day. "I plan to do (blank)." "Our plans include…" "What are you planning for (blank)?" We use the word so much that many people forget the importance of the actions required to bring a plan to life.

Challenges occur in every field or business. Wouldn't you rather be prepared for them? By creating a plan, you can respond to challenges that arise in real time. When developing your plan, it's important to include "what-if" scenarios. Stuff happens— things that are unexpected such as ups and downs in the market or the economy, changes in industry standards and environmental factors.

YOUR LEVEL OF PERFORMANCE DEPENDS ON YOUR LEVEL OF PREPAREDNESS

Planning gives you time to adjust your plan on your schedule and at your convenience rather than frantically altering your actions to adapt to changing circumstances. Updating and revising your plan regularly is also important.

Your level of performance depends on your level of preparedness. Through planning, you can see what next steps should be taken toward your goals and adjust your actions to stay on course.

Planning empowers you to:

// Be proactive

// Have time to adjust

// Improve performance

PLANNING FOR THE FUTURE

Who knows what the future will bring and how we should plan for it? In 1994, who could have known how big the Internet was going to become? Now more than 28 years later, most of our lives and jobs revolve around the Internet. In 1994, the Today Show's hosts, Bryant Gumbel and Katie Couric, contemplated the Internet during one of their morning programs. They questioned what the '@' symbol stood for and what exactly the Internet was.

Thanks to technology, things that we use daily in our lives are changing every year. You can now communicate easily with people from almost anywhere in the world thanks to smart phones. Medicine is personalized, and your television set is no longer a giant box with tubes. The things our children are growing up with did not even exist when we were their ages.

The times are changing, faster and faster. Are you being proactive or reactive to this change?

PLANNING IN REAL TIME—WHY IT WORKS

During the blackout that occurred in the middle of Super Bowl XLVII, Oreo took advantage of the incident to promote their product. "You can still dunk in the dark" became a legendary tweet. This tweet transformed the world of marketing—expanding the concept of instantaneous, real-time marketing.

Using real-time events to post and promote business activities online has quickly become a powerful development in social media marketing. Leaders and businesses are using current events and occasions that are trending to communicate with people, and people are responding to them, causing these messages to go viral in record time.

While no one can know exactly what surprises and developments the future holds, you can be ready for them. The key is planning. Use your imagination to create a vision of where you want to be and then create a plan for how you can get there. To begin, use The One-Page Marketing Plan in the Take Off section of this book. Planning and strategy can make all the difference in growing your brand and can make adapting to the future more manageable.

YOUR NUMBER ONE

CHALLENGE: Can you simplify your strategy into one thing? What is the number one thing you are focused on in your area of expertise right now? (just one)

// **NUMBER ONE:**

"IF YOU DON'T HAVE A COMPETITIVE ADVANTAGE, DON'T COMPETE."
— JACK WELCH

MESSAGING

FOCUS

CLARITY

STORYTELLING

FOLLOWERS

PROMOTERS

REPUTATION

PLANNING

BRAND

EDUCATE

MOTIVATE

AUTHENTICITY

WHAT'S THE NUMBER ONE THING YOU ARE FOCUSED ON? IF YOU HAVE A TEAM, DOES EVERYONE ON YOUR TEAM KNOW YOUR NUMBER ONE AND THEIR ROLE IN ACHIEVING IT?

BIG IDEAS

STAND OUT

PERSONA

VISION

NURTURE

ATTRACT

IDENTITY

DISTINCTION

THE ERA OF THE PERSONAL BRAND

Standing out has become increasingly challenging in a world of sensory and information overload. Despite this challenge, a familiar and trusted brand can still cut through the clutter. Thought leaders who look inside themselves to find the unique characteristics that differentiate them from the crowd can also stand out. Consider these trends when positioning yourself to stand out:

BRAND AWARENESS IS A KEY INITIATIVE:

// To stand out, you must have a clear idea of where you are standing now.

// Defining your key brand attributes (differentiation, relevance, promise and authenticity) will be important.

// Clarifying your core values, mission and vision will ground you in authenticity.

// What sets your brand apart will help establish your distinct advantage.

YOUR BRAND MUST ALIGN WITH YOUR STRATEGY AND PURPOSE:

// Brands have become increasingly disjointed and misunderstood.

// Your brand must be consistent with your identity, reputation and purpose.

// Alignment of these aspects will provide a firm foundation on which to build your strategy and direction.

BUILDING RELATIONSHIPS IS KEY:

// Intrusive mass-marketing is less effective than creating relationships built on trust.

// Focus on building long-term loyal relationships rather than short-term followers.

// Nurturing follower relationships will lead to greater top-of-mind awareness when people relate to the ideas or solutions you offer.

AUDIENCE EXPERIENCE REQUIRES DEDICATED RESOURCES:

// Positive follower experiences are crucial.

// Utilize technology to improve your follower's experience.

// Your audience has abundant choices (thanks to search tools and social networks) that make creating transparency and trust key to gaining and keeping followers.

// Audience experience should be a top priority for decision makers.

FOLLOWERS CONTINUE TO VALUE TRANSPARENCY:

// Followers seek higher engagement and demand transparency and honesty in what you say and do.

// Leaders need to "walk the talk" and create real value for their followers.

// If thought leaders do not tell the truth, someone else will do it for them.

// Transparency across all social and digital channels will foster trust and fuel long-term success.

// Genuine messaging should reflect brand alignment.

CONTENT REMAINS KING:

// Providing content based on followers' wants/needs builds trust and loyalty.

// Quality benefit-based content will increase search engine rankings.

// Content co-creation between leaders and followers will continue to be a top priority, creating value for the community where contributors are part of the process.

RESEARCH CONTINUES TO REMAIN A HIGH PRIORITY:

// Demand will increase for analytical apps like automated reporting, dashboards, predictive measurements and strategic support.

// 68% of leaders use research to enhance their audience's experience and improve process efficiency.

// Data will contribute to securing market intelligence.

USER EXPERIENCE IS CRUCIAL TO A ONLINE PRESENCE:

// As a first point of audience contact, websites must reflect the authenticity of your brand image.

// Google states the first impression of a webpage happens in the blink of an eye (50 milliseconds to be exact).

// 94% of consumers who rejected or mistrusted a website said it was due to design.

// Website development is now accessible to all levels of users because of the increasing options of pre-made templates.

VIDEO WILL CONTINUE TO BUILD BRAND EQUITY:

// 82% of all Internet traffic in 2021 was video; 15 times higher than 2017. (Source: Cisco and Biteable)

// 58% of individuals consider companies that produce video content to be more trustworthy, and 71% say that videos leave a positive impression. (Source: Animoto)

// 74% of marketers say video has a better return on investment than static imagery. (Source: Biteable)

// Engaging videos boost the chances users will stay on your website longer, increasing SEO.

MOBILE MARKETING IS NOT OPTIONAL:

// Optimizing your website for mobile is a necessity and a valuable investment.

// Optimizing and making the audience experience easier on a mobile webpage/app increases conversions by 160%.

// 45% of emails are opened on mobile devices. (Source: McKinsey's iConsumer survey)

// Mobile apps will outperform traditional ads as advertising and are preferred for their functionality. (Source: McKinsey's iConsumer survey)

// Users spend, on average, 82% of their time on mobile with apps and just 18% on browsers. (Source: Harvard Bus. Review)

LOCATION-BASED MARKETING CONTINUES TO RISE:

// The global location-based services market accounted for $36.35 billion in 2020, and is expected to reach $318.64 billion in 2030. (Source: Allied Market Research)

// Location data provides greater precision in targeting, more accurate tracking and insights for optimization.

// Interacting at the right place/time with value, affects audience decisions and fosters brand advocacy.

ONLINE ADVERTISING WILL SHIFT EVEN MORE TO MOBILE:

// 2021 was a record year for ad spending, with more growth expected in 2022. (Source: Forbes)

// U.S. mobile ad spending was up 23% in 2021 year-over-year, reaching $295 billion. (Source: Marketing Dive)

STORYTELLING = STORYSELLING:

// Zoom was one of the fastest growing apps of the the past 2 years; meeting participants increased by 2900%. As of February 2022, Zoom had 191,000 enterprise customers. (Source: Business of Apps)

// A recent study found the average human attention span has fallen from 12 seconds in 2000 to 8 seconds in 2021. (Source: Red Tree Communications)

// Slideshare and other visual presentation programs provide a visual/ interactive way to share.

// With the increase in social live feeds, real-time storytelling will increase.

// Infographics are here to stay to provide complicated information in a visually appealing way.

STANDING OUT IS HOW BRANDS WILL COMPETE:

// The global mediascape is making it more challenging to stand out.

// The New York Times estimated that a person living 30 years ago saw up to 2,000 ad messages a day, compared to between 4,000 and 10,000 in 2021. (Source: An-swerEGY.com)

// To stand out, you need to be more of what makes you who you are—authenticity.

// Identifying the elements of your distinct advantage and understanding how you are perceived will create a clear picture of the opportunities ahead of you.

(Year of the Brand Sources: ContentMarketingInstitute.com, SiriusDecisions "B-to-B Marketing Automation Study," Software Advice and Research Now "Demand Generation Benchmark," HubSpot, 5 IDC.com, Marketing and Management Sciences Book, Bright Local Consumer Review Survey, Google's Brand Lab, Animoto.com Survey (featured in NY Times, CNN, NBC, Bloomberg), EMarketer, NetElixir.com, Adestra Report On Top 10 Email Clients, Harvard Business Review, InboundNow.com, Huffington Post)

MARKETING TRENDS

MARKETING TREND EXERCISE: Which marketing trends influence your future growth and success as a thought leader?

// PRIMARY TREND TO FOCUS ON:

// MARKETING TRENDS:

- ☐ Brand Awareness
- ☐ Strategy Alignment
- ☐ Relationships
- ☐ Audience Experience
- ☐ Transparency
- ☐ Content
- ☐ Research

- ☐ Online Experience
- ☐ Social Marketing
- ☐ Video
- ☐ Mobilization
- ☐ Location Marketing
- ☐ Online Advertising
- ☐ Storyselling

// OTHER:

MESSAGE / BRAND STRATEGY ALIGNMENT

BRAND / STRATEGY ALIGNMENT: The goal is alignment. Start with the aligned goal, then explore independent strategies that complement and support each.

// MESSAGE STRATEGY:	// BRAND STRATEGY:

// HOW THE MESSAGE STRATEGY SUPPORTS YOUR BRAND:	// HOW YOUR BRAND STRATEGY SUPPORTS THE MESSAGE

// ALIGNED GOAL:

STRATEGY IN BRIEF:

// Strategy involves having an integrated set of goals and actions to reach those goals combined with the commitment to complete those actions.

// When your strategy is aligned with your purpose and brand, you are on course to achieve your goals.

// Creating a strategic plan and putting it in writing creates a baseline to measure your progress.

// Planning matters; by creating a plan you can respond to challenges in real time.

// Combining creative design with strategic action helps distinguish your ideas or solutions and further helps you to stand out. This is "hybrid thinking."

// Design influences an individual's decisions and is a source of competitive advantage for your brand and message.

// Your level of performance depends on your level of preparedness and your ability to respond through appropriate action

TAKE ACTION:

☐ Write a short list of the main goals you have for this month and how you will measure whether you achieved them or not.

☐ Make a similar list for this year.

☐ Write a short list of current trends that might help or hinder you from reaching your goals and what adjustments you might need to overcome those challenges.

FOCUS AND DISCIPLINE MAY WORK ON PAPER, BUT IT GETS HARDER WHEN YOU BEGIN TO IMPLEMENT AND ARE CONTINUOUSLY **DISTRACTED.**

I AM FOCUSED AND COMMITTED
TO ACHIEVING MY DESIRED RESULTS.

MINDSET

// IDENTIFY WHERE YOU STAND.

Which of these statements most accurately reflects your focus and commitment to achieve the desired results?

- ☐ I do not have a disciplined mindset.
- ☐ I have a somewhat disciplined mindset.
- ☐ I have a disciplined mindset, but I am not committed to achieving desired results.
- ☐ I have a disciplined mindset, I am committed to achieving desired results, but I am not focused.
- ☐ I have a disciplined mindset; I am focused, and I am committed to achieving desired results.

THROUGHOUT EACH WORKDAY, WE AIM TO ACHIEVE RESULTS. The more we have to deal with, the more our ability to focus is challenged. With distractions increasingly becoming a part of each day, even the most disciplined person can lose concentration and be side-tracked. **HOW CAN WE STAY FOCUSED ON WHAT NEEDS TO BE DONE TO ACHIEVE THE GOALS WE SET?**

Here are a few simple steps that work:

// Set goals. Setting goals that are specific, measurable, achievable, realistic and timely will help you commit to achieving your desired results. Setting goals will help you discipline yourself to see outcomes.

// Hold yourself accountable. Sometimes when we don't receive desired results it's because we make excuses. We don't "feel like it." Not allowing excuses is the first step to accountability. Holding yourself to a higher standard will help you reach the goals you set for yourself.

// Remove distractions. Distractions are one of the biggest reasons we lose focus. Without focused attention, discipline is impossible. Removing those things that will distract you from reaching your results will help discipline your mentality.

// A disciplined mindset is essential. And like anything else, practice makes perfect. Don't expect to become a disciplined mastermind within a day. Make lists, set reminders, and do whatever you need to do to keep yourself focused and accomplish the outcomes you want.

"WHATEVER THE MIND CAN CONCEIVE AND BELIEVE, IT CAN ACHIEVE."
— Napoleon Hill

"FOCUS ON YOUR GOALS, NOT YOUR FEAR."
— ROY BENNETT

WHAT DO YOU WANT TO ACCOMPLISH THROUGH YOUR MARKETING EFFORTS?

What types of media will you use to communicate? Do you want to drive traffic to your website, blog, or other social media site? Or do you want speaking engagements and public appearances? With your goal in mind, select a new strategy or adjust your current one accordingly, and then set a reasonable deadline.

Use Available Tools. Research the different tools available that you can use to measure social media data. You may notice the many companies that provide services for this type of measurement. After your research, pick the tools or services that will be most beneficial for your goals. You may already have access to some, like LinkedIn Analytics.

Watch On Your Own. While your networks are being measured, you can still play a part. Observe and monitor your social media channels. How is your audience responding to your messages? If you notice any problems, fix the issues and respond to the audience. Your awareness and attention may affect the measurements (in a good way!) in the long run.

Learn From Your Results. Your measurements should allow you to compare your results, to view your performance over time and to notice trends and what works or doesn't work. Use this information to fine-tune your strategy and message. Remember that online and social media are subjective and still growing, so there's no one definitive tool that will work for everyone the same. Your measurements should assist in tracking the progress you've made, so that you can continue getting the best results from your growth strategy.

MEASURING SUCCESS

Twins are always competing between themselves. With so much in common, they look for ways to outdo each other. One of the "competitions" between my identical twin sister Lorrie and I was simple—which one was the tallest? In the house where we grew up, we had a measuring tape on the inside of our bedroom door. Every so often, our parents would have us stand with our backs to the measuring tape, marking where the tops of our heads reached with a black marker. I'm sure every child has been measured like this at some point, but I had the pressure of being measured next to my twin. Lorrie was always just a little bit taller than me.

I desperately wanted to be taller, to win this "competition." I tried to stand as straight as I could during the measurements, but Lorrie always won, only by a little, but it was enough. I never quite caught up to her, but in the years since, I've learned that there are other, more important ways to measure growth and success.

In business and life, we often try to measure our success, which can be a vague and inexact process. Using analytics as a resource helps you measure your success in a more concrete way. Consider the goals that you set when you started using social media. Are you accomplishing what you wanted to, like driving more traffic to your website or building brand awareness? Metrics can help you see that answer more clearly.

The number of "likes" or "shares" that you get doesn't really tell you if your overall strategy is working—it's not an accurate measure of the success of your efforts. When you use specific tools for measurement, though, you will be presented with much more relevant information about your results. Different metrics tools will give you different information, like demographics on people who have liked your content, and how many people looked at your online presence may demonstrate which strategies are working, and which aren't. With this information, you can decide how to adjust your social marketing strategy.

We need to use analytics to measure our progress and success. These metrics help us know when we need to make changes and keep growing.

CREATING A DASHBOARD

Picture the dashboard in your car. You've probably glanced at it so many times that you have the layout memorized. Everything that you need to know when you're driving is right there, from your speed to your mileage, to the level of gas in your tank, to the "check engine" light that alerts you of a potential problem. You rely on the information your dashboard provides at a glance to keep you driving safely.

Dashboards are equally important online tools that can support your growth. These dashboards are organizational in nature. When you look at your online dashboard, you should see visual representations of your communications efforts. Dashboards can be customized to display what you think is most important or relevant to your efforts and your plan.

It's important that your dashboards are easy to understand. Whether their purpose is to condense a wealth of information into understandable graphics or charts, or to keep information easily accessible with less clutter, your dashboards should be clear and comprehensive. They exist for your own benefit, and since you typically get to choose what widgets or windows you see, you need to have them relatively organized. A dashboard can't help you much if you can't follow or understand it!

Ultimately, your dashboard should help you increase your productivity. Once dashboards have been set up to your liking, they should be a help, not a hindrance. Learning to navigate them may take time, but it will be well worth the effort. Following your trends, patterns, and metrics can tell you how to adjust your growth strategy, while making multiple updates to multiple networks through one tool can save you time and effort.

FOCUS.

"ANYTHING THAT IS MEASURED
AND WATCHED, IMPROVES."
— BOB PARSONS

WHAT'S ON YOUR DASHBOARD?

DASHBOARD: What's on your dashboard? What should be? Keep it simple—what metrics do you need to review on a daily, weekly, monthly and annual basis to stay on course?

// TRENDS:
- ☐ New Presentations
- ☐ Audience Referrals
- ☐ New Online Activities
- ☐ Off Radar

// CAMPAIGNS:
- ☐ Weekly Goal
- ☐ Monthly Results
- ☐ Annual Goal

// PLANNING:
- ☐ Monthly
- ☐ Quarterly
- ☐ Annual Summit

// AWARENESS:
- ☐ Website Visits
- ☐ Social Following
- ☐ Social Media Interactions
- ☐ Email Engagement
- ☐ New Followers

// WHAT'S ON YOUR DASHBOARD?

MINDSET

MINDSET EXERCISE: What new activities would be beneficial to start? What two things are you doing that are not working or are ineffective? What two things are you currently doing that are effective?

// START:

// STOP:

// CONTINUE:

MINDSET IN BRIEF:

// The more we must deal with each day, the more our ability to focus is challenged.

// A few simple steps to improve focus include setting goals, Holding yourself accountable, removing distractions, and maintaining a disciplined mindset.

// With your goals in mind, select a strategy, type of communication, the available tools and media, and then learn from your results.

// An online "dashboard" can help you condense diverse information into understandable and organized graphics or charts.

// How The One-Page Marketing Plan can help you organize your marketing and communications efforts.

TAKE ACTION:

- ☐ Write down one thing that you can you do today to increase your ability to focus and reduce your distractions. Then, do it.
- ☐ Tomorrow add another thing that you could do to reduce distractions and do that.
- ☐ Do this for five days.

MANY TIMES, WE CREATE A BIG IDEA, THEN WE GET STUCK ON THE RUNWAY BECAUSE WE ARE NOT CLEAR **ON WHICH DIRECTION TO TAKE OFF.**

☐ THE ONE-PAGE MARKETING PLAN
☐ OFF THE RADAR

TAKE OFF

// YOU HAVE ASSESSED YOUR STRENGTHS AND WEAKNESSES.

// YOU HAVE DEFINED WHAT YOU STAND FOR (YOUR PURPOSE).

// YOU HAVE ASSESSED PUBLIC PERCEPTIONS OF YOUR BRAND AND UNDERSTAND WHAT NEEDS TO CHANGE.

// YOU HAVE IDENTIFIED THE DISTINCT ADVANTAGES THAT DIFFERENTIATE YOU FROM YOUR PEERS AND YOU KNOW WHO YOUR BEST AUDIENCE IS.

IT'S TIME TO TAKE OFF.

THIS IS WHEN YOU DECIDE NOT ONLY WHAT IT IS THAT YOU WANT TO STAND OUT FOR BUT HOW YOU WILL MAKE THIS HAPPEN. It's essential that you establish and control how you are perceived by your audience and others. This is in the works. What you need now is a plan of action. Here's a high-level one-page marketing plan that guides you to:

- ☐ Increase exposure of your authentic personality.
- ☐ Uncover big sky ideas.
- ☐ Build stronger relationships with followers.
- ☐ Communicate your unique qualities and differentiators.
- ☐ Align your messaging across various media.
- ☐ Focus your strategy to key activities that lead to specific results.
- ☐ Target and nurture your ideal audience.
- ☐ Build a high-level plan that can be measured.

THE ONE-PAGE MARKETING PLAN

THE ONE-PAGE MARKETING PLAN: Go to

www.StandOutasaThoughtLeader.com to download The One-Page Marketing

Plan. If you need help building your Plan, contact StandOut@TwinEngine.com.

// COMPONENTS INCLUDE:

- [ ] Purpose
- [ ] Distinct Advantage
- [ ] Brand Positioning
- [ ] Brand Persona
- [ ] What You Stand For
- [ ] Brand Traffic Radar
- [ ] Ideal Audience
- [ ] Big Sky Idea
- [ ] Growth Strategy
- [ ] Key Messaging
- [ ] Off Radar Opportunities
- [ ] Key Campaigns
- [ ] Take-Off Campaign
- [ ] Key Issues
- [ ] Top 5
- [ ] Your Number 1
- [ ] Wing Earners
- [ ] Quarterly Targets

- ☐ Read the book *Stand Out as a Thought Leader*. To order copies, go to www.StandOutasaThoughtLeader.com or Amazon.com.
- ☐ Take the Brand Traffic Control™ Assessment: go to www.StandOutasaThoughtLeader.com to assess what areas of "The 8 Fundamentals" you need to strengthen.
- ☐ Brand Intelligence: Review online intelligence relative to your brand and field of expertise.
- ☐ Competitive Intelligence: Review competitor intelligence of developments that affect your field and your goals.

THE ONE-PAGE MARKETING PLAN IS BOTH A TOOL AND A PROCESS. Developed by the team at TwinEngine, it provides the ability to organize the key components of a brand marketing plan based on the Eight Fundamentals of Standing Out in Business. These include: Purpose, Reputation, Visuality, Authenticity, Ideal Leads, Distinction, Strategy and Mindset.

As a tool, the instructional guidelines begin with The Brand Traffic Control assessment where you (and your team) will evaluate your current position in each of the essential components of standing out. Based on The 8 Fundamentals, the tool will help you conceptualize your organizational purpose and what you stand for, define your distinct advantage, define your ideal leads, develop authentic messaging, define your brand positioning in the mediascape, brand persona (both internal and external), the key issues you are facing in your field and off-the-radar opportunities you may be overlooking.

As a process, the brand truths you uncover will lead you to determine your number 1 goal and the top 5 initiatives that will take you to a Stand Out position. You (and your team) will define lead strategies, key campaigns with big sky ideas designed to help you take off, win followers, and reach quarterly targets.

The process is a dynamic one, not static. The plan is designed to be a baseline from which to start the process, but one which will be revisited, at least quarterly, to remain accountable and to stay on course. The system provides a basis and structure from which to align your business strategies and goals with your marketing efforts to get you where you want to go.

BRAND ✈ TRAFFIC CONTROL

THE ONE-PAGE MARKETING PLAN

PURPOSE

DISTINCT ADVANTAGE

REPUTATION

IDENTITY

PURPOSE

AUTHENTICITY

MINDSET

AUDIENCE

STRATEGY

DISTINCTION

BRAND TRAFFIC CONTROL ASSESSMENT

AUTHENTICITY // BRAND PERSONA

DISTINCTION // BIG SKY IDEAS

BRAND POSITIONING

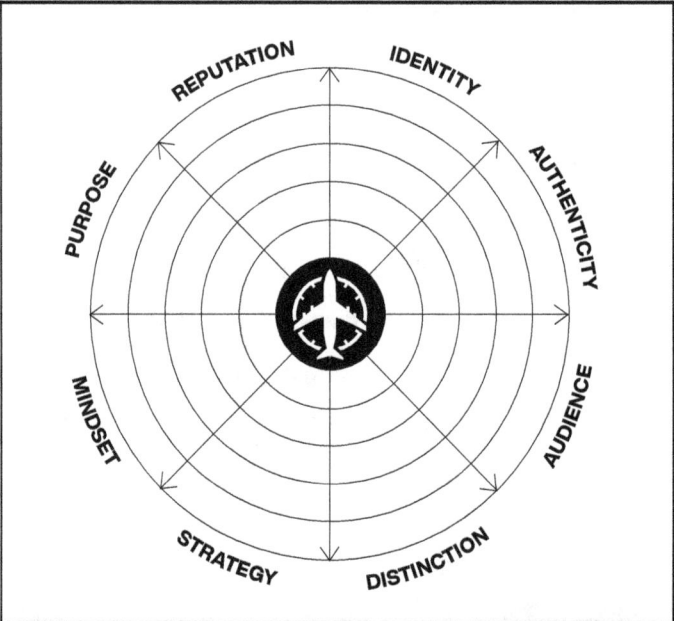

WHAT I STAND FOR

NEED HELP BUILDING YOUR PLAN AND IMPLEMENTING THESE TOOLS? GO TO WWW.TWINENGINE.COM //
© 1990-2022 TwinEngine. All Rights Reserved.

ORGANIZATION //	DATE //
NAME //	REVISED //

// TwinEngine™

AUDIENCE // PROFILE	STRATEGY // KEY CAMPAIGNS	STRATEGY // TOP 5
	THEME:	M - Q - A

AUDIENCE // STRATEGY	IDENTITY // TAKE OFF CAMPAIGN	STRATEGY // NUMBER 1

		STRATEGY // WING EARNERS
AUTHENTICITY // KEY MESSAGES	REPUTATION // KEY ISSUES	M - Q - A

	STRATEGY // KEY METHODS	STRATEGY // QUARTERLY TARGETS
		QUARTER //
OFF RADAR OPPORTUNITIES	1	1
	2	2
	3	3
	4	4
	5	5

STAND OUT **// 217**

1. BRAND TRAFFIC CONTROL™ RADAR

The Brand Traffic Control™ Radar is designed to assess the strength and alignment of your brand on The 8 Fundamentals of Standing Out as a Thought Leader: Purpose, Reputation, Identity, Authenticity, Audience, Distinction, Strategy and Mindset.

ACTION:

☐ Refer to the introduction or go to www.StandOutasaThoughtLeader.com to download the radar to plot your opinion of your current position within each indicator on a scale of zero in the center (non- existent) to five on the outside ring (highest level).

CHECKLIST:

☐ What areas need strengthening?

☐ Are the scores aligned on each of The 8 Fundamentals?

// NOTES

2. YOUR PURPOSE

Answer the questions below to gain a clearer idea of your purpose and how it fits into what you do.

// **What do you love?** What activities do you most enjoy?

// **What does the world need?** What do you do that adds value to the world?

// **What do you do really well?** What are your talents and skills?

// **How much does the world want and need it?** What do you do that others value and how much does the world want and need what you offer?

ACTION:

☐ Refer to the activities in the section on Purpose to discuss each of the aspects that lead to discovering your purpose. Share the outcomes.

CHECKLIST:

☐ My purpose is clear.

☐ I know what I stand for.

☐ My purpose is consistently communicated.

// **NOTES**

3. DISTINCT ADVANTAGE

Your distinct advantage is not just what makes you different, it's what makes your message different—when it's aligned with what you stand for and your authenticity. It is the unique combination of gifts, experiences, culture, stories, skills and inclinations that make up who you are and what you do in ways that others don't, can't and won't.

ACTION:

☐ Refer to the activities in the section on Distinction to discuss what your audience wants that you provide, and others don't. Use your findings to identify your distinct advantages.

CHECKLIST:

☐ I stand out in my audience.

☐ I stand out to my followers and influencers.

☐ I stand out among other thought leaders.

// NOTES

---

4. BRAND POSITIONING

Like a GPS directional device, our Brand Positioning Assessment shows you where you are relative to where you want to go.

// **Brand Differentiation**: How effectively does your brand capture the attention of prospects?

// **Brand Relevance:** How aligned is your brand to your followers' and prospects' needs?

// **Brand Promise**: How consistently does your brand deliver on its promises?

// **Brand Intelligence**: How well do you understand your brand and the quality and impact of the brand experience on your followers?

ACTION:

☐ To download this assessment to evaluate the current position of your brand go to www.StandOutasaThoughtLeader.com.

CHECKLIST:

☐ My brand is properly positioned.

☐ I understand what differentiates my brand.

☐ I leverage my brand equity.

// NOTES

5. BRAND PERSONA

When your story, messages and images reflect the values, beliefs, personality and lifestyle preferences of your audience, they'll feel more involved with you and your brand. And ultimately your ideas or solutions become an obvious choice as an extension of your story and your audience's needs and values. The key is authenticity—aligning what you communicate with who you truly are. If the personality you attempt to portray is just a façade, a mask for who and what you truly are, then your storytelling attempts to create an appealing personality will eventually fail.

ACTION:

☐ Refer to the activities in the sections on Identity and Authenticity to explore what words, images and personality traits create your brand persona.

CHECKLIST:

☐ Who you are on the outside is aligned with who you are on the inside.

// NOTES

6. WHAT YOU STAND FOR

Now, more than ever, your success is determined by how clearly you define and communicate your core values and qualities within your message. In short, it's all about what you stand for. What do you stand for? Whether you are well recognized in your field or not, you must know what you stand for before your audience can know. Do you know?

The question has become not only how can you stand out, but what will you stand for? It's crucial that you direct how you distinguish yourself in the national and global mediascape.

ACTION:

☐　Refer to the activities in the section on Purpose and Authenticity to explore how you communicate what you stand for to the world.

CHECKLIST:

☐　I know what I stand for.

☐　I consistently communicate what I stand for.

// NOTES

7. BIG SKY IDEA

What out-of-the box ideas can you launch that will take your brand awareness to big sky success? The media landscape is a crowded place. How can you get above the clouds to operate in blue skies and stand out from the crowd?

ACTION:

☐ Look for opportunities to improve and refine your message. Refer to the Big Sky Idea activity in the section on Purpose. Ask yourself these questions: What is the next idea that is going to take me to the next level? What big idea is going to help you stand out?

CHECKLIST:

☐ I think bigger and out-of-the-box when it comes to blue skies.

☐ I have a big idea that's going to take me to the next level.

// NOTES

8. AUDIENCE

The first step to create a flow of new followers is to agree on a set of criteria about what your best followers look like, then develop a profile to better focus your message and promotional efforts. The following are examples of information that you may include in your follower profile:

- [ ] A set of demographics that includes job level and seniority.
- [ ] A day in their life.
- [ ] A list of their pain points, motivations and goals.
- [ ] Where do they look for information?

ACTION:

- [ ] Refer to the activities in the section on Audience. Profile your ideal followers to understand their role, motivations and the challenges they face professionally and personally.

CHECKLIST:

- [ ] I know the characteristics and persona of my ideal followers.
- [ ] I have identified profiles for my target audiences.
- [ ] I know the behaviors of my audience and potential followers.

// NOTES

9. KEY MESSAGES

When your words match who you are and what you believe and your actions match your words, you are being authentic. Start with the question: "Who are you?" You are made up of layers. To be truly authentic, you must examine each of these layers until you reach the core of your beliefs, vision and goals. This is where you can clarify who you are and what you represent as a thought leader.

From there, every action and decision you make should reflect who you are. Your authentic self is a collection of all the things that make you unique and individual—your passions, talents, inclinations, life experiences and especially your values and beliefs— what you stand for and why you're in the field you're in.

ACTION:

☐ Refer to the section on Authenticity to explore what words, images and personality traits create your brand persona.

CHECKLIST:

☐ My messages are authentic and true.

☐ I know what people say about me and my brand.

// NOTES

10. OFF RADAR OPPORTUNITIES

What's missing in your field of expertise? Differentiation can come from filling a niche in your field that others have overlooked. What opportunities exist that may be outside your radar? Is there something missing that will take you to the next level to explore unchartered opportunities?

ACTION:

☐ Examine recent news and activities in your field and ask your followers. Refer to the activities in the section on Reputation.

☐ Look everywhere—including other related and unrelated fields.

☐ What problems in your field need solutions that you could provide?

☐ What frustrates you, your followers and others in your field the most that could lead to new solutions?

CHECKLIST:

☐ I have identified Off Radar Opportunities.

☐ I discuss Off Radar Opportunities at strategic planning sessions.

// NOTES

---

11 & 12. GOALS AND MEASUREMENT

KEY CAMPAIGNS:

☐ What are the top five communication activities you could use that align with your growth strategy?

TAKE OFF CAMPAIGN:

☐ How are you going to launch your Big Sky Idea?

KEY ISSUES:

☐ What are the key issues faced by other thought leaders and how do those issues impact your planned campaigns?

KEY METHODS:

☐ What are the key methods by which you will deliver your growth strategy?

TOP 5:

☐ What are the Top 5 initiatives that are going to help you Stand Out?

NUMBER 1:

☐ What is the number 1 thing (just one) that will be your focus each quarter of the next year?

WING EARNERS:

☐ What milestones/goals will you celebrate?

QUARTERLY TARGETS:

☐ What are your top 5 quarterly targets?

OFF THE RADAR

OFF THE RADAR EXERCISE: Bring together a diverse team of associates, followers, friends, etc. to explore ideas, then rate each idea on its impact and potential for success.

// WHAT IS MISSING IN YOUR FIELD OF EXPERTISE?

// WHAT PROBLEMS NEED TO BE SOLVED?

// WHAT DOES THE FUTURE LOOK LIKE:

THE ONE-PAGE MARKETING PLAN FOCUS

THE ONE-PAGE MARKETING PLAN FOCUS EXERCISE: What is your number 1 area of focus? How do the off the radar opportunities support it? What are the next steps and how will you accomplish each?

// NUMBER 1 AREA OF FOCUS:

// OFF THE RADAR OPPORTUNITIES THAT SUPPORT YOUR FOCUS:

// NEXT STEPS:

TAKE OFF IN BRIEF:

// Once you know what you stand for, you understand the public perceptions of your brand and understand what improvements are needed, once you have identified your distinct advantages and know who your best audience is, you are ready to "Take Off."

// The One-Page Marketing Plan is a helpful tool we created that guides you with your next steps.

// The Brand Traffic Control™ Radar is another tool designed to assess the strength and alignment of your brand and indicate which of The 8 Fundamentals need further development.

TAKE ACTION:

☐ Complete The One-Page Marketing Plan.

☐ Identify actions and prioritize where you need to bring other people into the process.

☐ Define how you will measure success.

☐ What is your number one area of focus?

YOUR GOAL IS NOT JUST OUT IN THE FUTURE; YOUR DAILY GOAL IS STAYING ON COURSE, STEADILY BUILDING YOUR BRAND AND **BUILDING BRAND EQUITY** AS WELL.

☐ BRAND TRAFFIC CONTROL™ CHECKLIST

STAY ON COURSE

// STAYING ON COURSE IS A DYNAMIC AND CONTINUAL PROCESS.

Over the course of your life, one or all of the 8 fundamentals could change at any time and for a variety of reasons. We encourage you to revisit the processes we have outlined in this book as part of your annual evaluation, strategy and planning.

To download a pdf, go to www.StandOutasaThoughtLeader.com to access the Brand Traffic Control™ checklist.

THE 90% RULE:

Before a pilot takes off on a flight, he creates a flight plan. He knows his destination and approximately how long it will take to get there. He lifts off at the scheduled time, but during the course of the flight, air turbulence, weather conditions, and other factors keep pushing the plane off course. In fact, the plane is off course about 90 percent of the time. 90%!

(Source: Stephen R. Covey, How to Develop Your Personal Mission Statement)

So, how does the pilot get to his destination on schedule? He gathers information regularly from his instruments, from radar and weather reports and from ground control technicians along the way. Using this data, he evaluates his current location relative to his destination and adjusts his direction to get back on course. In fact, he makes constant course corrections throughout the flight.

Becoming a thought leader is a lot like a pilot preparing to take off. You have a specific destination. You create a 'flight' plan, assemble the resources you need and begin your journey. But as you grow and become more well known, it's possible that the picture you envisioned as your destination has become less clear, overshadowed by the day-to-day details of the work. You are off course. And without a course correction, you might not reach your desired destination.

STAYING ON COURSE

Alignment is the unifying thread running through and connecting all The 8 Fundamentals. It is the overarching goal of Staying on Course and a dynamic situation for any leader. The 8 Fundamentals are a system, like a mobile. They work together and, under optimum conditions, they support and balance one another. But when one is deficient and out of balance, it affects the others. Likewise, an improvement in one that is deficient can make a significant difference in the others.

The overall effect of focusing on alignment of The 8 Fundamentals **is that it improves your performance more efficiently** than by focusing on any one fundamental alone.

BRAND TRAFFIC CONTROL™ CHECKLIST

Staying on course requires regular and consistent monitoring of The 8 Fundamentals that support continuing to Stand Out. This checklist is designed to assist in periodic evaluations. The statements define levels of accomplishment required to be on course. Unchecked boxes indicate areas needing improvement.

1. PURPOSE: You know and live your purpose; you know what you stand for and are true to your beliefs.

☐ **Purpose:** My purpose is clear, I know what I stand for, and I communicate my purpose consistently.

☐ **What I Stand For:** I know what I stand for and I consistently communicate it.

☐ **Stories:** Stories that support my purpose are documented and shared.

2. REPUTATION: I monitor my brand perception, trends within my field and the current mediascape.

☐ **Key Issues:** I stay updated on the key issues that are relevant and timely to my field of expertise.

☐ **Brand Chatter:** I monitor weekly what is being said about my brand, my ideas and communications.

☐ **Industry Chatter:** I monitor weekly trending topics and news related to my field.

☐ **Competitive Monitoring:** I monitor what is being said about my peers and other thought leaders.

3. IDENTITY: The outward appearance of my brand truly reflects who I am and the value I deliver.

- ☐ **First Impression:** The outward appearance of my brand truly reflects who I am and the value I deliver.
- ☐ **Consistency:** My brand is presented consistently on all channels and across all media.
- ☐ **Brand Survey:** I survey my brand annually to assess its strengths and weaknesses.
- ☐ **Monitoring:** I monitor how my brand is expressed and I have a response plan in place.

4. AUTHENTICITY: My messaging is consistent, true, genuine and communicates my value propositions.

- ☐ **Key Messages:** My key messages are defined, shared and continuously updated.
- ☐ **Authenticity:** My key messages are genuine.
- ☐ **Value Propositions:** I have defined and share my primary and secondary value propositions.
- ☐ **Voice:** My brand voice is defined and consistent in all my communications.
- ☐ **Elevator Pitch:** I can consistently respond to the question 'What do you do?'

5. AUDIENCE: A consistent funnel of new followers is nurtured and managed.

- ☐ **New Follower:** My strategy is defined to nurture and manage new and existing followers.
- ☐ **Preferred Passengers:** I can identify my best followers and know their profiles, motivations and behaviors.
- ☐ **Brand Persona:** My brand persona addresses the demographics, psychographics and motivations of my best prospects.
- ☐ **Stowaways:** I know how to identify high maintenance / low value followers.

6. DISTINCTION: Stands out in a field of expertise, among audiences, influencers and other thought leaders.

- [ ] **Big Sky Idea:** I have defined the big idea that sets me apart from others in my field.
- [ ] **Protected Air Space:** I have identified the areas in my field in which I have significant advantages.
- [ ] **Distinct Advantage:** I have defined the distinct advantage that separates me from others.
- [ ] **Take Off Campaign:** I develop and launch an annual 'Take Off' theme and campaign.

7. STRATEGY: A strategy is in force and aligned with my goals

- [ ] **Marketing Plan:** A plan is in place and updated quarterly.
- [ ] **Alignment:** My communication plan is aligned with my strategic plan and core initiatives.
- [ ] **Annual Planning:** I identify my marketing initiatives for the year.
- [ ] **Brand Equity:** The methods to deliver my brand are leveraged.
- [ ] **Editorial Calendar:** I maintain a monthly messaging strategy and editorial calendar.

8. MINDSET: Focus and commitment to achieve desired results.

- [ ] **Number 1:** My number 1 priority is defined and updated quarterly.
- [ ] **Disciplined Mindset:** I have focus and a disciplined mindset.
- [ ] **Top 5:** I identify my top 5 growth initiatives and monitor them monthly.
- [ ] **Brand Standards:** My brand is clearly defined and my brand standards are up to date.
- [ ] **Off The Radar:** I stop quarterly to explore unchartered areas for exploration and growth.

BRAND TRAFFIC CONTROL™ CHECKLIST

BRAND TRAFFIC CONTROL™ CHECKLIST SUMMARY: What is my number 1 Fundamental that needs strengthening? What are my top 5 areas that need improvement?

// NUMBER 1 FUNDAMENTAL THAT NEEDS STRENGTHENING:

// TOP 5 AREAS THAT NEED IMPROVEMENT:

STAY ON COURSE IN BRIEF:

// Staying On Course is continual process of evaluating which of The 8 Fundamentals needs adjustment to continue your steady growth as a thought leader.

// We recommend revisiting the processes in this book as a part of an annual evaluation and strategic planning practice.

// Alignment of The 8 Fundamentals improves your performance more efficiently than focusing on any one fundamental alone.

// Use our convenient worksheets and Brand Traffic Control™ Checklist to evaluate your process.

TAKE ACTION:

☐ Complete the Brand Traffic Control™ Checklist.
☐ Look for areas to improve.
☐ Identify the number one fundamental that needs strengthening.

STAY ON COURSE IN BRIEF:

// Staying On Course is continual process of evaluating which of The 8 Fundamentals needs adjustment to continue your steady growth as a thought leader.

// We recommend revisiting the processes in this book as a part of an annual evaluation and strategic planning practice.

// Alignment of The 8 Fundamentals improves your performance more efficiently than focusing on any one fundamental alone.

// Use our convenient worksheets and Brand Traffic Control™ Checklist to evaluate your process.

TAKE ACTION:

- [ ] Complete the Brand Traffic Control™ Checklist.
- [ ] Look for areas to improve.
- [ ] Identify the number one fundamental that needs strengthening.

READY?

// NOW THAT YOU HAVE KNOWLEDGE OF THE FUNDAMENTALS OF WHAT IT TAKES TO STAND OUT AND THE SPECIFIC TOOLS TO TAKE YOU TO THE NEXT STEP, WILL YOU TAKE IT?

☐ I am not ready.

☐ I am somewhat ready.

☐ I am ready, but I am not committed to the process.

☐ I am ready, I am committed to the process, but I am not focused.

☐ I am ready, I am focused, I am commited to the process, and I am committed to standing out as a thought leader.

WILL YOU MAKE THE EFFORT TO DEFINE YOUR PURPOSE? And differentiate yourself by identifying your distinct advantage? Will you take the steps to align who you are with what you do and use the power of your authenticity to distinguish yourself in your field? Looking at where you are now, does it all seem overwhelming? **OR HAVE YOU ALREADY DONE THE WORK NEEDED TO ALIGN YOUR EFFORTS AND STAND OUT?**

We wrote this book to help thought leaders gain a unique perspective on how they can stand out. It's meant to introduce tools and resources to help you define who you are (distinct advantage), clarify how you represent yourself to prospects and followers (brand) and align these in practical ways to achieve specific measurable goals (strategy).

These concepts and exercises are specifically structured to uncover what is missing in your promotions plan. They are also designed to help you become more of who you already are and inspire you to become the success you were destined to be.

It can be overwhelming to try to keep track of how and if you are being noticed and followed. How can you know with any certainty if your brand is on course or lost among the crowd?

Brand Traffic Control™ is designed to provide you with a new way of aligning your brand. Using straightforward tools, it shows you how to strengthen and master The 8 Fundamentals of Standing Out. When you strengthen them, your brand will stand out; you'll know where you are relative to others in your field; you'll know how to create consistent messaging for your followers and prospects to increase engagement; your brand will be in alignment; you'll be able to execute plans more effectively; you'll know what makes your brand distinct; you'll have a tool to measure what's working and what isn't; and, you'll be able to position your brand to take off.

5 THINGS TO DO TO START STANDING OUT

Thank you for reading our book! If you need support or a facilitator to guide your strategic plan implementation, we're here to help—StandOut@TwinEngine.com.

Here are the 5 things you can do now to start standing out, today!

1. READ AND SHARE THIS BOOK:

☐ **Download the executive summary** — www.StandOutasaThoughtLeader.com

☐ **Share the book with others** — Collaborate on areas of focus.

☐ **Top 10 take-aways** — Identify your top 10 take-aways and next steps.

2. TAKE THE ASSESSMENT:

☐ **Take the Assessment** — www.StandOutasaThoughtLeader.com

☐ **The 8 Fundamentals** — Know where you stand and what fundamentals need strengthening.

3. ALIGN YOUR PROMOTIONAL STRATEGY AND BRAND STRATEGY:

☐ **Read the section on Strategy**

☐ **Brand / Strategy Alignment Exercise** — Refer to the exercises in the Strategy section.

☐ **Get Aligned** — Start with the aligned goal, then explore independent strategies that complement and support each.

4. DISCOVER YOUR DISTINCT ADVANTAGE:

☐ **Read the section on Distinction**

☐ **Discover Your Distinct Advantage** — Refer to the exercises in the Distinction section.

5. PLAN YOUR STRATEGY SUMMIT:

☐ **Read the sections on Strategy and Take Off**

☐ **Set a Date** — Plan a full day strategy summit.

☐ **Complete The One-Page Marketing Plan** — Refer to The One-Page Marketing Plan instructions in the Take Off section.

REMINDER: TO BE MORE. **BE MORE OF YOU** AND NOT ANYONE ELSE. IN TODAY'S WORLD, IT'S THE SUREST PATH TO STANDING OUT, TAKING OFF AND STAYING ON COURSE.

ABOUT THE AUTHORS

Winnie Hart and Lorrie Lee bring 35+ years of experience leveraging their twin talents (left brain/right brain thinking) consulting with leaders and businesses to help build and grow their brands to stand out. It starts with defining what they stand for and the difference they make in the world. They then take left-brain, strategic activities like core value proposition, data analysis and sales strategy and apply them to right-brain activities like big ideas, visual strategy and authentic messaging to create an aligned brand and business strategies.

At TwinEngine, a brand growth agency fueled by purpose, we believe that everyone has a distinct advantage that, when discovered, provides just the inspiration and momentum to reach their destination.

Winnie and Lorrie are also the authors of *Stand Out—Mastering The 8 Fundamentals of Standing Out in Business* and *What Do You Stand For?*. They are also the creators of The One-Page Marketing Plan and Brand in the Box™—strategic tools to help brands build a clear, structured plan to stand out, take off and stay on course.

PRAISE FOR **WINNIE HART AND LORRIE LEE**

// Winnie and Lorrie have built a go-to guide that will help any emerging thought leader to figure out not just what their message is, but how they can get their message out in a crowded market. Run, don't walk, to get yourself a copy of this definitive roadmap if you want to make a difference and build a business that has an impact.
—**JOHN CORCORAN** – Co-Founder, Rise25 LLC, Rise25.com

// One of the most compelling definitions of strategy I have read comes from Michael E. Porter's article "What Is Strategy" in Harvard Business Review; simply put strategy is "what makes you different". In a crowded arena of business and leadership-related books, Winnie Hart's courage to be herself and only herself, and her book *Stand Out as a Thought Leader,* stands out for not only does each and every page embody the idea of "what makes you different", Winnie guides the reader step-by-step through how one can differentiate themselves from the noise and from their competitors. And in a world with so much noise and information, the ability to truly stand out and be celebrated for our differences is what gives us a complete, competitive advantage. Read this book and have a bias towards action; you won't be disappointed.
—**KYM HUYNH** – CEO at HFGROUP, Founder at Executive Assistant Institute, Founder at WeTeachMe, President Emeritus at Entrepreneurs' Organization, Author at The Forum Formula, KymHuynh.com

// Winnie Hart is first and foremost an Entrepreneur Thought Leader! I believe entrepreneurship is the number one change agent in the world. It creates jobs, innovates products, and, most importantly, impacts people's lives every single day through the products and services we create. Everyone should use Winnie's experiences to find their own authentic space of thought leadership.
—**PATRICK BRYANT** – Co-Founder & CEO, CODE/+/TRUST. CodeAndTrust.com

// In today's world, it's easy to get lost in the barrage of content. As leaders, we are so fortunate to have a tool as authentic and impactful as *Stand Out as a Thought Leader* to help guide the path and support us in standing out from the noise. This book offers clarity and helps bring purpose to light in 8 actionable fundamental ways. Whether we need to incorporate all 8, or hone in on the one you need, *Stand Out as a Thought Leader* is a book we all need on our shelves to refer to time and again. Winnie and Lorrie, thank you for helping me with my message and for clarifying my purpose.
—**KATTY DOURAGHY** – President, Artisan Creative, ArtisanCreative.com

// Have you ever wondered what it would take to be a thought leader? To share your thoughts and your content for an audience that is excited to hear from you? *Stand Out as a Thought Leader* by Winnie Hart is the book you need to take you from wondering to doing. Creating a reputation as a thought leader isn't about putting content out there and hoping someone likes it. It's a thoughtful process that creates a trust between you and your audience. Winnie outlines the strategy and the steps needed become a thought leader in a sea of voices. You'll learn the eight vital areas that contribute to your success and create your own thought leadership platform.

—**ANDREA HEUSTON** – CEO & Founder of Artitudes, Host of *The Lead Like a Woman Show* Podcast, Artitudes.com & LeadLikeAWoman.biz

// *Stand Out as a Thought Leader* is an exceptionally well written and well organized book that I truly enjoyed both reading and applying to my own life. Unlike many other leadership books I've read, this one stands out for it's easy to understand fundamentals to becoming a thought leader who is genuine, purposeful and authentic. Winnie and Lorrie brilliantly share their extensive expertise in a way that goes beyond traditional principles of branding and present their content in a fresh and engaging format. Many AHA moments that have helped me stand out as a thought leader, as a speaker and coach. I highly recommend it!

—**MICHELE HECKEN** – Founder, Alpha Global Experts Inc, a division of Michele Hecken Executive Coaching, MicheleHecken.com

// Print this out and tape it to your refrigerator. Winnie and Lorrie know how to authentically capture what a person stands for and how to attract people to it. Their expertise is not fluff. They apply rigor to complex scenarios and the results are unique and impactful. This book includes easy-to-follow exercises and practical advice for those who want to do this work on their own. I highly recommend for anyone with a mission that requires humans to land.

—**CHRISTINA HARBRIDGE** – Mischief Executive Officer, Allegory, Inc., Allegoryinc.com

// *Stand Out as a Thought Leader* supports personal branding through purpose and authenticity. In today's environment, developing one's personal brand as a leader or entrepreneur is no longer an option; it's a necessity. Winnie's book provides valuable tools for the experienced or budding leader to help them accurately define what their purpose is and how they can best communicate it to their audience.

—**SUSAN DRUMM** – CEO, Chief Empowerment Officer, Meritage Leadership Development, MeritageLeadership.com

// Are you looking for a partner to help you focus and message not only who you are, but what you aspire to be? We were fortunate to have such a partner in Winnie and Lorrie when we embarked on a complete rebrand and messaging project to reposition our organization to be fit for purpose. The team helped us focus on the future, who and where we wanted to be, how we were going to get there and the lasting message that helped us stand out as the thought leader in our industry. Their efforts were critical to our success that we are now experiencing and the messaging that is resonating with our team, partners, and future partners as we grow.

—**CHUCK BAUMAN** – Chief Executive Officer, Inspire, InspireSolutions.com

// By segmenting the broader concept of thought leadership into 8 easy to under-stand sections, Winnie and Lorrie have created a successful process that simplifies everything. The reader is guided via a series of integrated exercises that move from discovering one's purpose, developing authenticity, and setting an intentional mindset. This book should become an essential component of any leader wanting to put in the time and effort to work on themselves!

—**JAMIE DOURAGHY** – Best-Selling Author, *On Guard and On Point: Mastering the Duel Between Life and Work*, JDouraghy.com

// More than a book, *Stand Out As a Thought Leader* is a guided transformation jour-ney. Straightforward, motivating, and action-oriented. It reads as if they are speaking just to you. Winnie and Lorrie are the real deal. If you hunger to spread your wings and take off as a thought leader then Winnie and Lorrie are the coaches you need and *Stand Out as a Thought Leader* is the playbook to help you soar.

—**CONOR DONAHUE** – Chief Operating Officer, Inspire, InspireSolutions.com

// Winnie's message is incredibly powerful and timely. Today, we live in a world where business leaders are expected to promote positive change. In her book, Winnie cap-tures the true driver that makes such change possible: purpose. Combined with a con-scious leadership style anchored around authenticity, purpose is the key to making an impact beyond maximizing profits at all cost.

—**KENT GREGOIRE** – CEO, Symphony Advantage, SymphonyAdvantage.com

DEAR LEADER,

More than ever, the world needs you to stand out as a thought leader and live your purpose. Are you willing to take a stand and stand out?

THE WORLD NEEDS YOU.

www.ingramcontent.com/pod-product-compliance
Lightning Source LLC
Chambersburg PA
CBHW082005190326
41458CB00010B/3078